MEASURED DRAWING FOR ARCHITECTS

MEASURED DRAWING
FOR ARCHITECTS

Robert Chitham

The Architectural Press: London

Dedication

To my wife and family, who whenever called upon, without demur hold onto the other end of the tape.

First published in 1980 by The Architectural Press Ltd: London

ISBN: 0 85139 391 8 (hardback edition)
       0 85139 392 6 (paperback edition)

Photographic acknowledgments
The photographs listed are reproduced in this book by kind permission of the following:-
The British Architectural Library: 1–3, 6, & 9–13. (Photos: Geremy Butler Photography).
The British Architectural Library Drawings Collection: 4, 5, 8, 14, 16 & 46. (Photos: Geremy Butler Photography).
The Trustees of Sir John Soane's Museum: 7 & 15. (Photos: Godfrey New).
The Greater London Council: 19–21, 38, 39 & 51. (Photos: 51 Godfrey New, remainder GLC).
The Royal Commission on Historical Monuments: 22 & 23.
The National Monuments Record: 24, 25 & 30.
The Historic American Building Survey, National Park Service, US Department of the Interior: 26 & 27 (Photos: Brian Piper).
The Photogrammetric Unit, Institute of Advanced Architectural Studies, University of York, on behalf of the Directorate of Ancient Monuments and Historic Buildings, Department of the Environment (Crown Copyright): 28 & 29.
The University of Nottingham: 50.
Richard D. Grasby: 65.

Printed in Great Britain
by W & J Mackay Limited, Chatham

CONTENTS

PREFACE

In 1978 the Measured Drawings Competition, sponsored jointly by the paper manufacturers Wiggins Teape, the Victorian Society and the Architects' Journal stimulated considerable interest, prompting the entry of over 500 drawings by 116 competitors. On the conclusion of the competition, which demonstrated that there is considerable interest in the subject of architectural measured drawing, I was asked by the publishers to write a book on the topic, about which the existing literature is surprisingly scanty.

There seem to me to be two quite different aspects of the subject, those of history and current practice, and I hope that my separate treatment of the two has not resulted in too obvious a division of the book into two disparate parts. The more I looked into the history of measured drawing, the more difficult a subject I found it to cope with. Measured drawing has not generally, it seems, been regarded as a separate topic in its own right, but simply as a subsidiary part of the whole business of architectural drawing. Now architectural drawing and draughtsmanship is, of course, the universal sub-stratum of the whole subject of architectural history, and as such would represent a daunting subject for a single book. I have therefore deliberately been very selective, at the risk of offending the purists, and have confined myself almost entirely to the consideration of drawings intended for dissemination or publication.

The review of contemporary techniques of measured drawing has been quite a different and in a sense a much easier matter. Here I have endeavoured as far as possible to avoid the discussion of architectural drawing techniques in general, and keep fairly closely to matters which directly affect the production of measured drawings of existing buildings.

During the process of writing the book I have learnt a great deal both about measured drawings and about writing books! Perhaps the most important thing I have learnt is the degree to which the writing of a book depends on the help and advice of a large number of people. In future, I shall I hope be less prone to skim over the acknowledgements with which all books containing actual information are certain to begin. I should like to thank Mr David Dean, the Director of Library Services of the British Architectural Library, and Mr John Harris, the Curator of the Library's Drawings Collection, and their colleagues, as well as Sir John Summerson of the Sir John Soane Museum and Mr Nicholas Cooper of the National Monuments Record, all of whom gave me great help with the illustrations. My thanks are also due to Mr Ross Dallas of the Institute of Advanced Architectural Studies at the University of York, for information and illustrative matter on photogrammetry. I am especially grateful to Mr Ashley Barker and his collective mine of information in the Historic Buildings Division of the Greater London Council, in particular to Messrs John Earl and John Sambrook for help with illustrations, to Mrs Vanessa Brand for valuable advice on the text of the historical summary, and Mr John Fidler for information on American and Canadian practice. I have had helpful correspondence with Mr Max Bourne, Director of the Australian Heritage Commission, Mr Paul Stark of South Australia, Mr Peter Staughton of Victoria and Professor Douglas C. Rhyn of the University of Wisconsin. My thanks also to my wife for patiently vetting the text, to Mrs Judy Piper for typing it, and to the owners and occupiers of various buildings of which drawings appear in this book.

I INTRODUCTION: THE PURPOSE OF MEASURED DRAWING

My first introduction to the techniques of measured drawing was in the field of architectural model-making. This, and some youthful attempts at archaeological reconstruction stood me in good stead when I embarked on a career in the architectural profession. In the first practice I joined I was called upon to assist in a number of alteration and restoration jobs, and a degree of competence in measured drawing techniques helped me not only with the measured surveys I was required to carry out, but also with acquiring a familiarity with the three dimensional form of the buildings with which I was concerned.

Drawing is the primary language of architects. Writing, the fundamental means of communication, is quite inadequate in the technical context of architectural practice. A complete written description of a building is inevitably very long-winded, as every writer of specifications knows. Length defeats clarity, but any attempt to reduce it breeds ambiguity. Moreover, it is very difficult, confronted with the long written description of a building, to visualise the whole thing. As you read on, the beginning of the description fades. It is difficult to check back without losing the thread, and so on.

Drawings, coupled with written description (either separate or in the form of annotations), overcome these problems. A well-presented plan enables you to study the construction of a building in minute detail, in the context of the whole. The exact relationship of the parts can be instantly understood, symmetry and the hierarchy of spaces immediately appreciated, materials and finishes comprehended. It is therefore important that everyone engaged in the practice of architecture should be able to draw, at least with precision and preferably with elegance.

Normally, architects are primarily engaged in formulating designs in the form of drawings, and then supervising the translation of these drawings into three-dimensional buildings. But if the most efficient way of describing a building that is yet to be constructed is by means of drawings, it follows that drawings are also the best means of recording a building which exists. Much can be done with photography, but drawings have considerable advantages over photographs. They do not suffer significantly from distortion, they are not at the mercy of vagaries of the light, and they can be produced to any degree of detail which is considered appropriate. Thus design drawings and working drawings precede the process of construction, whereas measured drawings are the re-translation of an existing building into two-dimensional form. Four main purposes may be identified for carrying out measured drawings, namely measured surveys for alteration work, the recording of buildings before demolition, the scholarly production of exemplars, and the training of students.

The preparation of a measured survey of an existing building which is to be altered is an essential preliminary to any alteration job, and the more accurate and thorough the survey the easier the subsequent work will be. Floor plans and sections are equally important, especially where new staircases or the construction of new multi-storey buildings adjoining the existing are contemplated. Accuracy of dimensions, including the thickness of external walls, partitions and floors, is essential, and the rectangularity of rooms and the levels of floors should always be ascertained. Not only does a high degree of precision at this stage enable the designer to make assumptions about the alterations with confidence – whether staircase layouts are feasible, or whether kitchen or bathroom equipment will fit into the spaces allocated – but a great deal is learnt about the nature and construction of the building you are dealing with. Deep floor thicknesses in old buildings, for instance, suggest compound floor-construction, while measuring the thicknesses of partitions, coupled with 'sounding', gives an immediate clue to their construction, whether of stud or brick. Excessive thickness of external brick walls in old domestic buildings may mean that the brick is a later facing on a surviving timber frame, and so forth. Moreover, beyond the indications of constructional details which can be derived from measuring, more general attributes of buildings can be established. I know of instances in which the disparity of visible dimensions led to the discovery of supplementary staircases concealed within the thickness of walls. Indeed, the very fact of spending time in a building making a methodical measured survey of it will establish a sympathy with it and a mastery of its secrets which will facilitate the process of planning and designing alterations, and will help to ensure that these alterations are sympathetic in their nature. Successful architectural work is very much dependent on attention to detail, and this attention deserves to be paid at the survey stage as well as subsequently.

Buildings represent a sizeable proportion of the constructive endeavour of man. They are inherently costly in terms of resources, and they tend to be long-lived. They form much-loved reference points and navigational 'fixes' in people's lives, and they tell us a great deal about their way of life, their customs and aspirations. It is not generally in dispute, therefore, that the recording of buildings which are to be demolished is worthwhile. Different buildings deserve a different degree of recording depending on their significance, but however limited the record, it is of assistance if drawings form part of it. Indeed, the type of measured survey that I have suggested should precede alteration work, would be most appropriate for recording purposes too. It may be that somewhat less attention can be given to the details of construction – except where these are themselves of archaeological interest, such as the timber joints in medieval barns – whilst the elevations, and the profiles of mouldings need more emphasis. In general, however, the same tenets, of accuracy and systematic measurement, apply. The ultimate aim should be, I suppose, that with the aid of the measured drawings of a demolished building, supplemented by photographs, an accurate facsimile could be built. This level of recording can seldom be attained, nor is it invariably necessary. The plan-form, general elevational appearance and section, and the relationship with adjoining buildings, are of particular concern.

Measured drawing for the purpose of providing exemplars is perhaps considered of less significance today than it has been in the past. I shall touch in my historical summary on the developing search for standards of architectural beauty which led Renaissance architects, and subsequently the exponents of the Gothic Revival in England, to the production of measured drawings of every ancient building of note and many that are obscure. There has been a tendency in the architectural profession in more recent years, to disregard historical precedent and in every new design to try to make a fresh start from first principles. However, in a humbler but perhaps no less useful form the exemplars continue to be published – few editions of architectural magazines appear without some pages devoted to drawings of working details of new or existing buildings. Thus architects continue to pass on their information on the fundamentals, such as keeping the wet out, preventing walls from cracking, retaining warmth and keeping out cold – not simply in structurally appropriate ways, but also with sophistication of design.

Lastly, there is the business of student training. As I have said, it is important for everyone in architectural practice to be able to draw, in order to be fluent in the architect's primary language. It is surprisingly difficult for the layman, or for the student embarking for the first time on a course of study in architecture, to appreciate from the start the essence of the three-dimensional nature of buildings. This is clear from the efforts of the intelligent layman to draw buildings. Such basics as the overhang of eaves, the reveals of windows and doors, the very solidity of buildings, seem not to be commonly observed. Whilst, therefore, a student should start from the outset to make his own designs, it is not uncommon for these initially to display the same ignorance of construction, the same lack of structural commonsense.

As a corrective to this lack, the preparation of measured drawings is most useful. Students can quite rapidly become familiar with the three-dimensional nature of buildings by measuring them,* and a whole host of subsidiary benefits flow from this kind of practical study. Obvious examples are a knowledge of historical form, especially of detailing, the common sizes of components such as brickwork, windows, staircases, doors, as well as methods of construction, framing of roof-trusses and direction and spacing of floor joists. All these vital items of the architect's stock-in-trade can be painlessly assimilated whilst the student gradually acquires fluency in draughtsmanship.

* I have not reached any firm conclusion as to whether measuring should be carried out in imperial or metric dimensions, and cannot claim to be consistent throughout the book on this matter. The reasons for this apparent vacilation are discussed in part III 3c. (page 22).

II HISTORICAL REVIEW

Drawings of buildings, however slight, give clearer and more permanent ideas than can be obtained from the most detailed, correct and elaborate descriptions. Sir John Soane, 'Royal Academy Lecture 1' 1809.

1 The Renaissance

The foundation of architectural development is the book. Architects who desire to push forward the frontiers of progress in design, faced with the difficulty of finding patrons willing to realise their expensive innovations in bricks and mortar, have habitually rehearsed and refined their ideas on the printed page. Historians have just as habitually analysed the work of architects and sought to define standards of excellence. But just as drawing may be claimed to be the primary language of contemporary architectural practice, so study of the literature of history reveals the inadequacy of the written word unsupported by illustration.

Thus Leone Battista Alberti (1404–72) complained that the Roman architectural writer Vitruvius 'wrote in such a manner that to the Latins he seems to write Greek, and to the Greeks Latin, but indeed it is plain from the Book itself that . . . he might almost as well have never wrote at all, at least with regard to us, since we cannot understand him.'[1] Most of Vitruvius is stodgy, and some passages are so obscure that scholars have been arguing over their meaning ever since the Renaissance. To a large extent though, the difficulty of interpreting Vitruvius stems from the absence of illustrations in the manuscript texts which survived until the invention of printing in the mid-fifteenth century. 'If the noble and useful arts of Engraving and Printing had been known to the Greeks and Romans' said Soane to his students 'what treasures we should now possess. . . . Vitruvius would not have been left to his commentators; we should have had his full thinking.'[2]

The perfecting of printing with movable type made possible the widespread dissemination of architectural thought, but the precision in the transmission of technical information afforded by the illustration of books required two further steps. First, the very need for such precision had to be recognised. For authors of the early Renaissance as for their predecessors, the purpose and value of illustrations was judged on other criteria than that of accuracy of delineation, nor were they averse to filling gaps in the available evidence by recourse to imaginative invention.

Second, the earliest illustrators of printed books were trapped within the limitations of the medium of reproduction available. In the middle of the fifteenth century, printed books were produced from *xylographica* – whole pages containing both text and illustrations printed from a single woodcut. When the development of movable type made redundant the production of text by these laborious means, the woodcut survived in the printing craft as the only method of producing illustrations. Now a woodcut is prepared by patiently paring away the background of a block to leave a relief design capable of transferring ink to the page by surface contact. This process, whilst it lends itself to a wide range of rich artistic expression, is of its nature by no means ideal for the preparation of technical drawing. The criteria for this kind of drawing are clarity, precision, ease of repetition, to facilitate the efficient transmission of information rather than aesthetic content. However skilled the craftsman in woodcut might become, to meet these criteria the engraving, in which the ink is drawn onto the page from a groove in the parent plate – known as *intaglio* – is superior. It allows for accurate setting out and measurement, neat annotation, and the precise repetition of thickness of line which can be mechanically produced.

Thus Serlio's five-part *Book of Architecture* published from 1537 onwards is the first great illustrated treatise of its kind to make extensive use of measured drawings, and at the same time archaic in relying on woodcuts for their reproduction. A. E. Santaniello, writing of Serlio in 1970, states 'The sketches and finished plans in the third book set a standard that would become the object of emulation in architecture books for the next century'[3] (plate 1). Subsequent authors may well have striven to approach his standard of draughtsmanship, but his medium, the woodcut, was now gradually abandoned. The earliest surviving book of any kind printed with metal engravings dates from 1477. It took another sixty or seventy years for the process of engraving on both metal and wood to become firmly established in the printing trade, but once it became commonplace, architectural writers were in a position to disseminate their thoughts in written and pictorial form with as much exactitude as their skills at writing and drawing allowed.

And this they proceeded to do, in growing numbers. The whole process of Renaissance architecture is counterpointed by a continuo of architectural writings, by Scamozzi, Peruzzi, Vignola, Palladio in Italy, by de l'Orme, Perrault in France, by Campbell, Kent, Gibbs, Chambers in England. What did they write about? Predominantly, taking their cue, as Alberti had done, from Vitruvius, they attempted to deal with three broad subjects. First they wrote about the whole vast range of practical problems encountered in building, from town planning and the siting of buildings to construction, materials, the seasoning of timber and the calibration of sun-dials. Second they dealt with the matter of building planning, with the location, scale and orientation of different kinds of building and of their constituent parts. Third they wrote, tirelessly, about aesthetics and the search for standards of beauty. Naturally, different writers disagreed widely over the extent to which such standards could be established, but all averred that limits could be identified within which systems of proportion in design are especially satisfying aesthetically, and most went on to indicate how such systems could be enhanced by decoration.

These writers searched specifically in two places for evidence of the parameters of aesthetic excellence. Many sought corollaries in the field of music, attempting to apply the criteria of musical harmonics to the preparation of standards of visual proportion. The second source of evidence was the surviving stock of buildings of antiquity, wherein it was assumed that the standards were already embodied, so that their measurement and comparison would provide an appropriate set of criteria. Therefore, Renaissance writers were overwhelmingly and ever-increasingly concerned with the study of ancient buildings and the derivation from them of rules for drawing the five Classical orders. This obsession with the orders which is the core of Renaissance architectural development is evident from the titles of books spanning across three centuries of architectural theory: *Regola Delli Cinque Ordini d'Archittetura* by Vignola (1562); *Rules for drawing the Several Parts of Architecture* by James Gibbs (1732); *Nouveau Parallele des Ordres* by Normand (1819) (plate 3). Architectural writers were at pains to measure the buildings of antiquity, both for their own edification and to support the theories they developed about the criteria of design. The doyen, Alberti, insisted on the importance of learning from antiquity: 'There was not the least remain of any ancient structure, that had any merit in it, but what I went and examined, to see if anything was to be learned from it.'[4] In the mid sixteenth century Palladio set himself to 'search into the reliques of all the antient edifices . . . and . . . with the utmost diligence to measure every one of their parts'[5] (plates 4 and 5). Nearly two hundred years later again William Chambers was at it, preparing to write about the Orders having 'measured with the utmost accuracy . . . many ancient and modern celebrated buildings, both at Rome and in other parts of Europe'[6] (plate 8).

Alas, whilst many authors seek to assure us of the diligence and accuracy of their measured work, few make any allusion whatever to the way they went about it. Technical drawing has clearly been consistently regarded as so humble a craft, so secondary a means to an end, that our knowledge of its methods and techniques can best be derived from the study of surviving drawings, supplemented by rare instances of written information. Sir Roger Pratt, writing in 1660, gives as valuable an insight into drawing techniques as anyone.[7] He writes of the preparation of 'Royal or Imperial Paper' as a substitute for parchment or vellum, and the need to smooth it with 'an ivory slicker', and discusses drawing with black lead pencils, 'the blackest and least brittle whereof are the best, or with ink . . . either Indian, which is the most secure from blotting, or common, which we must be sure to have neither too white nor too thick . . . quills, which must not be too far slit, for fear of too hastily shedding the ink, or of brass, which are generally so sharp that they somewhat cut the paper.' He deals with the rule, the compass and the square – 'but one who understands but little of Geometry will do well enough without it' – and describes how drawing paper, as large as possible, should be pinned to the board.

Perhaps the most interesting aspect of the subject to emerge from Pratt's notebooks is the arbitrary nature of scales for drawing at that date. The scale of a particular drawing was determined solely on the basis of choosing the largest scale to which the subject could be accommodated within the confines of the sheet of paper selected. The actual scale of each drawing was prepared individually by means of a simple scale-rule having a large number of graduations to the inch, any convenient number of these graduations being used to represent one foot. Clearly the evolution of standard scales for drawings came later.

Apart from the lack of standard scales, draughtsmen had other problems to contend with, and other drawing conventions. They could neither trace nor print, and the cost of materials called for frugality. Drawings were usually set out on a grid, scribed, rather than drawn, upon the surface of the paper, the finished drawing being superimposed in pen or pencil. Copies were made by pricking through the significant junctions of lines from one sheet to another, a laborious process fraught with opportunities for error. While much Renaissance drawing is most meticulous, detail was often very sketchily treated, presumably on the assumption of a degree of familiarity on the part of the reader with the minutiae of decoration and enrichment.

In spite of these limitations, architectural writers strove for accuracy in their research, and certainly claimed it for the results. Palladio in the preface to his *Four Books* emphasises 'the labours that I have from my youth hitherto undergone, in searching and measuring (with the greatest care and diligence I could) all those ancient edifices that came to my knowledge.'[8] Isaac Ware, in the Advertisement to his 1737 translation of the same work endorses the accuracy of the illustrations by reference to attempts 'to copy his excellent and most accurate wooden prints on copper plates.'[9]

At the same time this vaunted accuracy was frequently impugned by later writers. In the late seventeenth century Colbert sent Desgodetz from Paris to 'measure Roman antiquities with accuracy'; in the resulting *Edifices Antiques de Rome* (plate 6), Desgodetz took every opportunity of pointing out the inaccuracies and errors perpetrated by Palladio; only to have his own errors posthumously exposed by Soane in his Royal Academy lectures, with particular reference to his rendering of the Temple of Vesta at Tivoli: 'The building affords many proofs of the inaccuracy of Desgodetz, which it is the more necessary for me to notice to prevent the young artist from placing too great a confidence in his representations, which he might be led to do, from observing every page filled with pointing out the errors of those who preceded him'[10] (plate 7).

Of the Italian architects Palladio was easily the most influential on the English (plate 2). The copy of the *Four Books* annotated by Inigo Jones (and now in the possession of Worcester College, Oxford) attests to the directness and intensity of the architectural lineage. As the British Isles expanded into the architectural sophistication of the eighteenth century, of which Jones was the herald, so the volume of architettural literature and illustration grew. Under the patronage of such men as Lord Burlington, Colen Campbell (d. 1729) produced from 1717 onwards his great collection of drawings *Vitruvius Britannicus*. In the first two volumes, thirty three out of the two hundred plates were of his own projects, and thus not strictly measured drawings, but the remainder showed a wide range of taste, including examples of work by Vanbrugh (though little of Wren or Hawksmoor) as well as by Jones (plate 9).

On the other side of the political fence, James Gibbs (1682–1754) published in 1728 the *Rules for Drawing the Several Parts of Architecture* in which the whole edifice of the orders was boiled down into a neat mathematical system in which 'all fractions, in dividing the principal members and their parts, are avoided' (plate 10). Clear and elegant as Gibbs's plates may be, others were less certain that the orders could be so simply encapsulated. As long ago as 1674 Perrault, in the foreword to his translation of Vitruvius, had declared that 'Beauty has hardly any other foundation than *fantasie*.

It is up to human agencies to furnish (rules) and in order to do so a definite authority, taking the place of reason, should be generally agreed to.' Eighty years later, Sir William Chambers (1726–96) questioned the need for such an authority – 'Perfect proportion is simply a visually pleasing relationship between the objects in a composition'[11] – but still felt sufficiently confident to illustrate his *Treatise Upon Civil Architecture* (1759) with drawings of ideal orders. Chambers was only one of the army of British architects of the eighteenth century whose apprenticeship included a protracted visit to the continent, and especially to Italy. Indeed it was practically *de rigeur* for young Englishmen of any substance to embark upon the Grand Tour, and for those who intended to make architecture their profession the culmination of the trip was in Rome. Chambers, Taylor, Dance, Ware, Adam – all, from their own resources or through patronage, found their way to Rome, and seem to have used their time there diligently, not simply gaping mindlessly at the grandeur surrounding them, but minutely examining, surveying and measuring the antiquities.

All this activity could not but make for a steady increase in scholarship and standards of accuracy. Robert Adam's stay in Rome, in particular, coincided with the publication in 1756 of Piranesi's *Le Antichita Romane*, a massive survey of the remains of the City which went considerably beyond the bald recording of surface form and dimension into an examination of building construction, planning and decoration, all presented in an arresting visual manner (plate 11). At the same time, ease of communications coupled with a straightforward desire to investigate hitherto undisturbed sites, led to a gradual widening of the geographical range of buildings being studied and becoming familiar to the generality of architects. The crowning result of this was the growth of interest in the antiquities of Greece. In fact, as early as the 1680s, while Desgodetz laboured over his Roman notes, Francis Vernon 'gazed on the Parthenon' and 'took all the dimensions with what exactness he could.'[12] In 1739 Lord Sandwich, a founder-member of the Society of Dilettanti 'measured the principal Athenian monuments and produced creditable ground plans and a few brave elevations.'[13] The first detailed drawings were to come ten years later from the pen of Richard Dalton.

Scholarly inquiry into the ancient architecture of Greece came of age in 1762 with the publication of the first volume of *The Antiquities of Athens* by Stuart and Revett. This series, also inspired by the Dilettanti, was to run to six volumes over the course of the next sixty years. The appearance of the first volume, two years before the Adam brothers' *Ruins of the Palace of the Emperor Diocletian at Spalatro in Dalmatia*, provided the ammunition for argument over the respective merits of Greek and Roman precedent, which was eventually to become very polarised, becoming, by the end of the century, a 'Battle of the Styles' (plates 12 and 13).

2 The age of revivals

At the same time, however, material was beginning to be accumulated for what seems to us a much more fundamental battle than that between Greek and Roman, namely that between Classical and Gothic. In England in the seventeenth and eighteenth centuries interest in the wealth of Gothic buildings which survived was sporadic. Interest in Gothic cannot be said to have died out altogether at this time, as has often been inferred, although the condition, for example, to which Westminster Abbey Chapter House was reduced during its period of service as the Record Office shows a lamentable disregard for architecture, and for Gothic architecture in particular. Regard for Mediaeval buildings, as distinct from Gothick fancy, was certainly confined to the few. Of them, easily the most important was James Essex (1722–84), who spent most of his working life in Cambridge, employed on the restoration and extension of numerous University buildings. He was an assiduous antiquary and recorder of old buildings who extolled the virtues of Gothic, especially of vaulted roof-systems. He insisted that in order to understand Gothic buildings fully 'time must be spent in measuring their parts'. His detailed notes and drawings, have, alas, never been published, but he paved the way for the spread of serious recording and analysis of Gothic which in the early nineteenth century eclipsed the argument between Greece and Rome as the central point at issue between revivalists. This was an age of profuse and meticulous book-illustration. Thomas Bewick (1753–1828) revived and improved the technique of wood-engraving towards the end of the eighteenth century, and the craft of steel and copper-engraving developed to meet commercial demands for illustrations. Thomas Rickman (1776–1841) expanded the classification of Gothic styles propounded by Essex half a century earlier, and invented the terminology of Early English, Decorated and Perpendicular still in everyday use. His book *An Attempt to Discriminate the Styles of English Architecture from the Conquest to the Reformation*, first published in 1817, demonstrates how many craftsmen were at work in the field at that time, as well as the extent to which the author called on others to illustrate his theories. The book is profusely illustrated indeed, with measured drawings and details, perspective views and diagrams. Later editions contain no less than 400 illustrations contributed by at least fifty artists and engravers, fewer than thirty illustrations being by Rickman himself (plate 14).

As the nineteenth century got into its stride, the debate over the propriety of historical architectural style became less a matter of intellectual controversy between scholars, and took on more the appearance of a holy war. Armed by now with the fruits of the labours of Rickman, Britton and others, as well as the familiarity with mediaeval architecture arising from the studies encouraged by his father, Augustus Welby Pugin (1811–52) declared Gothic architecture, and especially Early English, to be the only style appropriate to the design of churches. Repeatedly, in such books as *Contrasts* (1836), and *The True Principles of Pointed or Christian Architecture* (1841), Pugin hammered home his message of 'fitness of purpose', equating Gothic with Christianity and Classical with Paganism. The message is reinforced with cartoons and with measured drawings. Though in many cases disappointingly slight (in view of Pugin's virtuosity as a draughtsman) they represent a marked shift in the purpose of the measured drawing, from an adjunct in a search for an intellectual ideal to a kind of religious polemic.

The nineteenth century not only saw the maturing of the idea of morality in Architecture; it was an age of systemisation. The emergence of the professional man called for the proper regulation of architectural education. The prototypical system, the Ecole des Beaux Arts, had been founded as long before as 1671 as the Academie Royal d'Architecture, by Colbert, Minister to Louis XIV. Its function evolved as a search for universal principles of Architecture, based on the study of Classical examples. From 1780 onwards, students were required to make a detailed study of the ancient building of their choice. The yearly competition, the concours du Grand Prix de Rome was emulated by the Royal Academy in London from the mid-eighteenth century onwards. Perhaps the most distinguished Royal Academy silver medallist was Sir John Soane (1753–1837), with drawings (presented in 1772) of Inigo Jones's Banqueting House. Soane subsequently became the most famous of the Royal Academy's Architectural lecturers. His meticulous analysis of the orders and review of architectural history presented in two series of lectures from 1809 onwards were illustrated by a magnificent sequence of rendered drawings, on the grandest scale, including not only large numbers of measured drawings, but also many perspectives which Soane considered necessary to explain the buildings fully (plate 15).

The Soane lectures influenced a whole generation of architects, not least among whom was C. R. Cockerell (1788–1863), himself in turn a distinguished lecturer, and in 1860 the first architect President of the Royal Institute of British Architects. Cockerell, who had made considerable antiquarian studies in Greece and Asia Minor, was a skilled draughtsman, and in particular measured the temple of Apollo at Bassae, containing the earliest known example of the Greek Corinthian Order (plate 16). He had little time for the equation of Gothic architecture with Christianity, regarding it as humbug. He criticised Ruskin and others for wanting only one style – 'Romano-Catholic plan adapted to a Protestant ritual – buttressed walls with tie-beam roofs, belfry towers without bells, and all the quackery of sedilia, piscina etc. where they are without use or purpose'.[14]

As the century progressed, the text-books and the drawings proliferated. In 1874 Phene Spiers published his book *Architectural Drawing*. Spiers was himself educated at the Ecole des Beaux Arts, admired the French draughtsmen Normand and Letarouilly, and thought the French system of education infinitely sounder than the English pupillage system in which 'study in architectural drawing . . . must perforce . . . be attempted in a haphazard manner, having to be almost invariably undertaken by the pupil in his own leisure time after office hours, and being sometimes entirely neglected until the Articles are terminated.' His book was clearly intended to bring hope and enlightenment to the poor pupil, and is a very down-to-earth primer, dealing with all aspects of drawing, and setting down principles for the draughtsmen – standard colours for materials in section, for example – many of which are familiar today. The section on measured drawing is brief but contains much useful information, from the establishment of horizontal and vertical datum lines and the estimation of height to the taking of moulding profiles using soft copper wire.

At the turn of the century, Reginald Blomfield, perhaps more important as an architectural writer than as a designer, made it obvious that he detested the Gothic revival – 'the amateurs, on the strong current of the romantic movement, carried the day, and have retarded the development of architecture in the country by at least a hundred years'[15] – and that he was heartily glad that this unseemly episode was now over. He saw the influence of the Beaux Arts in what he detected as a gradual improvement in draughtsmanship in the first years of the twentieth century, and recognised a direct link between competence in drawing and competence in design. Blomfield suggested two essential conditions of measured drawings, first that they should be perfectly accurate, and second, that they should be perfectly clear.

Publications of measured drawings from the end of the nineteenth century reflect the loss of conviction in the historical styles which preceded the birth of the Modern Movement. An immense amount of measuring and recording was done, both in this country and abroad, but much of it appears to be intended primarily as an advertisement for the draughtsman, or as an extensive but amorphous quarry for the busy eclectic architect. Not that the quality of the work was at fault; the drawings in Mervyn Macartney's *Practical Exemplar of Architecture*, for example, bear out the compiler's claim to provide 'indispensable memoranda for more leisurely and intensive study' than can be gained from inspecting the building on the site (plates 17 and 18). Perhaps the most astonishing (and overlooked) individual collection of measured drawings prepared from this time onwards for educational purposes is in Sir Banister Fletcher's *History of Architecture on the Comparative Method* first published in 1896.

3 Contemporary practice

Whilst the confidence of architects in the reinterpretation of historical style faltered, concern for the preservation of historic buildings became more articulate. The Society for the Protection of Ancient Buildings dates from 1877, and the Ancient Monuments Protection Act from five years later. An early practical consequence of this concern was increased interest in the production of measured drawings purely for record purposes. The Committee for the Survey of the Memorials of Greater London was formed in 1894, to 'watch and register what still remains of beautiful or historic work in Greater London, and to bring such influence to bear from time to time as shall save it from destruction or lead to its utilisation for public purposes.'[16] Its first illustrated monograph, prepared by C. R. Ashbee and published in 1896, took as its subject the Trinity Hospital in Mile End (plate 19), and is the first and honourable ancestor of the monumental *Survey of London*, now undertaken by the Greater London Council, a parish-by-parish account compiled from both documentary and architectural sources, and profusely illustrated by measured drawings and photographs, (plates 20 and 21). Interest was not of course confined to London. In 1908 the Royal Commission on Historical Monuments was established, and charged with the compilation of inventories of Historic Buildings throughout the country. It set out to record every building dating from before 1714, as well as to make recommendations as to which buildings were worthy of preservation, a task which perhaps makes that of the *Survey of London* seem relatively easy to encompass. Like the *Survey of London* it embarked on the publication of this massive inventory on an area-by-area basis. Though strictly logical, this process made no allowance for the inevitable reduction in the number of ancient buildings surviving in the country as a whole during the very long time span necessary for the whole of the book to be completed (plates 22 and 23).

When to this 'natural' wastage of historic buildings were added the depredations caused by aerial warfare, concern at the slow rate of progress of the Royal Commission led in 1941 to the establishment of the National Monuments Record under Walter Godfrey. This was designed not only to accommodate records of post 1714 buildings, which failed to qualify for inclusion in the Royal Commission volumes, but also to serve as an ever-expanding data-bank of visual records of old buildings, both photographic and drawn (plates 24, 25, 30). The National Monuments Record remained independent of the Royal Commission until the early 'sixties, at which time the administrations of the two bodies were to a large extent amalgamated. At about the same time, in response to increased public anxiety over the losses of old buildings, the recording of buildings faced with demolition became a specific responsibility. The National Monuments Record now contains the largest single collection of architectural measured drawings in the country, including the bulk of the measured drawings previously held by the Drawings Collection of the British Architectural Library.

Other countries have followed suit. In the United States the methodical recording of buildings pioneered before the turn of the century received much impetus from Federal Relief Funds projects set up during the depression. In 1933 the National Parks Service of the Department of the Interior inaugurated the Historic America Buildings Survey, and the embryo project was buttressed by the passage of the Historic Sites Act 1935 which authorised the Secretary of the Interior to 'secure, collate and preserve drawings, plans, photographs and other data of historic and archaeologic sites, buildings and objects'. A large part of the survey work is now carried out by local amenity and history societies, and by architectural students. A high level of co-ordination is maintained by the professional officers of the Service, and the work of the survey is reviewed by a national Advisory panel including historians and members of the American Institute of Architects. Buildings are recorded by a combination of drawings, including photogrammetric surveys, photographs and written data, and completed surveys are lodged in the national archive in the Library of Congress (plates 26 and 27).

In Australia, under the aegis of the Australian Heritage Commission, responsibility for recording buildings of interest rests generally at the State rather than the Federal level. Arrangements for the maintenance of records vary somewhat from State to State. In Victoria, the Historic Buildings Preservation Council requires measured drawings and photographs to be kept of most buildings threatened with demolition, whilst the most extensive records are maintained in the Public Record Office and the Latrobe Library, both in Melbourne. In South Australia the Heritage Unit and the National Trust are primarily responsible for recording, records being lodged in the State Archives.

The recording of buildings by means of measured drawings is a recognised part of architectural students' training throughout Australia. In Victoria, techniques of both recording and presentation are encouraged by the annual Matthew Flinders competition, which has become an acknowledged part of the Melbourne architectural year. The use of photogrammetric recording techniques is pursued in a number of places, including the Department of Surveying, University of Melbourne, and the South Australian Institute of Technology.

4 Photogrammetry No major changes seem imminent in the basic techniques of drawing and measuring buildings, although it is worth noting that the first phase of the Canadian Inventory of Historic Buildings, launched in 1970, is specifically devised as a comprehensive computer-record of the salient physical characteristics of each structure of interest. There is, however, one field in which advances in technology have recently come to the aid of the building surveyor. This is the process of photogrammetry and its derivatives.

For a number of years it has been possible to take 'square-on' photographs of buildings and by enlarging them to a precisely determined size to use them as the basis of scale drawings. Whilst a reasonable approximation can be achieved with an ordinary camera, not all the distortion introduced into the picture by vertical perspective can be eliminated in the enlarging process; a rising-front camera overcomes this difficulty. Clearly this technique has limitations, in that it is only of value for measuring extensive, planar elevations, and even in these, recessions and projections produce errors.

True photogrammetry, developed from aerial mapping techniques, relies on exploiting stereoscopic cameras built to a very high degree of precision, of known optical characteristics, the photographs from which are used in a special plotting machine to draw the elevations. Although it requires sophisticated equipment and specially trained operators, photogrammetry offers a swift and highly accurate method of surveying large areas of elevations, and is especially advantageous where traditional surveying methods would require elaborate means of access (plates 28 and 29).

NOTES

1 Alberti, *De re aedificata VI.I*. Facsimile of Leoni's 3rd edition of 1755, Tiranti, London, 1965.

2 Soane, 'Royal Academy Lecture l.' Soane's *Lectures* ed. Arthur Bolton, Soane Museum Publication 14, London, 1929.

3 A. E. Santanello, Introduction (p. 10) to facsimile of *Serlio: The Book of Architecture* New York, Benjamin Blom Inc., 1970.

4 Alberti, *De re aedificata VI.I*: as note 1 above.

5 Palladio, preface to *I Quattro libri dell'Architettura*. Facsimile of Isaac Ware's English edition of 1738. New York, Dover, 1965.

6 Chambers, *Treatise on Civil Architecture (1759)* quoted by John Harris, *Sir William Chambers*, p. 138, London, A. Zwemmer, 1970.

7 Pratt, *Architectural Notebooks 20.11.1660* (MS L 31.44V) ed. R.T. Gunther, Oxford, O.U.P., 1928.

8 Palladio, as note 5 above.

9 Isaac Ware's 'Advertisement' of his 1737 edition of Palladio, as note 5 above.

10 Soane: 'Royal Academy Lecture II', as note 2 above.

11 John Harris, *Sir William Chambers*, p. 137, as note 6 above.

12 J. Mordant Crook, *The Greek Revival*, p. 5 London, John Murray, 1972.

13 Ibid, p. 7.

14 C. R. Cockerell: on 'Style in Architecture' reported in *The Builder* Vol. 7, p. 337, 1849.

15 Blomfield, *Architectural Drawing and Draughtsmen*, pp. 85–6, London, Cassell, 1912.

16 C. R. Ashbee, *The Trinity Hospital in Mile End: Note of the Committee for the Survey of the Memorials of Greater London*, London, Guild and School of Handicraft, 1896.

III MEASURING ON THE SITE

Thus I was continually searching, considering, measuring and making draughts of everything I could hear of. Leone Battista Alberti, *De re aedificata, VI.I.,* (1485).

1 **Introduction**

Whenever I am faced with a task involving prolonged concentration and a sustained standard of accuracy, I find myself going through a preliminary phase in which I waste time on all kinds of pretexts to put off starting serious work. This procrastination takes all sorts of quite trivial forms, such as fussing about providing a superfluity of long, sharp pencils, renewing backing sheets on drawing boards, or walking out to post letters despite the knowledge that the post has gone.

I do this so consistently and so compulsively, that I have come to suppose that for me at any rate it is a necessary process, a kind of mental adjustment which I have to undergo in order to achieve the right frame of mind to make a satisfactory start on the work.

In the case of surveying a building, this moment of mental re-tuning can be turned to good effect. It is a good idea, on arriving on the site, rather than plunging in immediately to plot plans, sections and elevations, to devote a few minutes to walking round the building, making a preliminary assessment of it. You may find it best to do this in an entirely informal and subjective way, merely aiming at absorbing some of the 'feel' and character of the place. More objectively, you can go through a checklist of essential characteristics, pace the overall dimensions, estimate overall and floor-to-floor heights, try to establish the date of origin and major subsequent alterations, note construction and materials, and assess the extent to which details are repeated. Work out in broad form the scope and number of the drawings you will need to produce adequate records for your purpose.

This kind of preliminary assessment will help you to plan the course of the measured survey, save you from unproductive repetition of detailed work, and from false starts in plotting the building.

2 **Equipment**

The first architect I worked for used to reminisce about his own early experiences as the pupil of Sir Reginald Blomfield. He carved out a small niche in the office as the man who drew up surveys. One morning, arriving at the office he met the great man on the point of departure, who instructed him to draw up a particular measured survey carried out at the weekend. Going straight to examine the survey notes he found them entirely dimensioned not in feet and inches but in terms of 'B'. Rushing out after the departing architect, he called out: 'What are all these dimensions – 3B, 6½B and so on?' Sir Reginald waved his umbrella and called back: 'I measured it all with my brolly.' To which he intelligently replied: 'Well, leave your brolly behind – I've no idea how long it is!'

Choice of equipment for measuring is to a very large extent a matter of personal choice. Whilst few will be satisfied that accurate site surveys can be produced with no more equipment than an umbrella, a balance has to be struck between making sure you have all the things you need, and being so overloaded with equipment that it becomes unmanageable. Drawing materials and equipment are so well covered in books on draughtsmanship such as Fraser Reekie's exhaustive *Architectural and Building Graphics* that a blow-by-blow introduction to the drawing board and tee-square would be superfluous, so it is really a question of identifying those weapons in the draughtsman's armoury that are going to be the most use on site.

To some extent this will depend on the method of on-site survey adopted. You will need somewhat more elaborate equipment if you are going to plot the measured drawing as you go, than if you are to dimension a freehand sketch and develop the measured drawings back in the office. I shall return to the advantages of these alternatives later; on the premise that before you go to the site you must first assemble your materials for survey, I shall discuss the selection of these first.

a Drawing boards For either method the first requirement is for paper and drawing board. If you are to site-plot a building of any size, this means you will be in effect setting up a simple drawing-office on the site, for which obviously you need a drawing board, of at least A2 and preferably A1 size, complete with backing sheet and of course with a tee-square of appropriate size, and an adjustable set-square. For sketch plans, something considerably smaller and more manageable may be preferred. The limits of size, which can only be learned by experience, are on the one hand, how small a drawing you can accurately annotate, so that it can subsequently be translated, and on the other hand, how big a sheet of material you can handle standing on the top rung of a ladder in a gale. Maybe two sketching boards should be prepared. A board of A3 size is fine for sketching plans on terra firma, but once I get to any height, to draw tracery detail for example, all I can handle is something of about A4 size.

Not only must you select a board of manageable size and light weight – ³⁄₁₆ plywood with smoothed edges makes a good material for sketching boards – but you must decide how to fix the paper on it, again bearing in mind that the wind is a powerful enemy when you are measuring outside. Clips and drafting tape are both useful, though the one sometimes gets in the way of the drawing at one end of the board, while the other makes drawings almost too immobile, which is a nuisance when you want to refer to more than one sheet during a session. Probably rubber bands at each end of the board provide the neatest and most flexible way of securing the paper. In addition, I have often thought that an extra small board, provided with a couple of hooked straps so that it could be clipped over the rung of a ladder, would be of great help, but I have so far lacked the energy to make one.

b Paper I have made site sketches on all sorts of papers, ranging from feint ruled foolscap to heavy cartridge. It is as well to choose paper that is fairly tough, partly because it may receive fairly rough treatment, and partly because (unless you are much more meticulous than I am) you will need to do a fair amount of rubbing out. Furthermore, a lot of site measuring is surprisingly dirty work, and a paper that rapidly becomes ingrained in dirt will not allow the clearest drawings. It is therefore important that the paper should not be too soft-surfaced; moreover a spongy surface, like that of a lot of cartridge papers, requires a soft pencil, and soft pencils need frequent resharpening. The other consideration is whether you find lines on grids helpful in initial freehand setting out.

My own preferences would be as follows: for simple surveys, especially where it is convenient to file the survey in an ordinary job file, prepunched ruled A4 sheets are adequate. The ruling helps in producing a rapid, well-proportioned drawing, and the pad itself forms a makeshift drawing board. For proper survey work, I use layout paper, either A3 or A4. This is fairly densely surfaced, but thin enough – the pad in front of me is 45 gsm in weight – to be partly transparent. This means I can mount it on the board over a sheet of squared paper which shows through sufficiently to serve as a reference grid for setting out.

c Media
For most surveys I think the use of pencil is essential. Even if you make no mistakes in setting out or dimensions, a shower of rain will rapidly undo good work executed in ink. The grade of pencil you use is a matter of experience and personal taste. The important thing is to choose a grade which on the paper of your choice maintains a firm, clear line as long as possible. Loss of clarity in either drawing or annotation leads to ambiguity, but it is irritating to have to keep sharpening a pencil. Because it is easier to sharpen, a clutch-pencil is probably preferable to a traditional wood pencil, although through sheer habit I usually use the latter – it can be embarrassing, however, searching in someone else's immaculately kept sitting room for somewhere to hide pencil shavings, whilst a little graphite dust alone is readily dispersed even in such surroundings.

I do, however, make limited use of coloured felt pens in measuring. When plotting a survey in the office, I indicate on the site drawings in colour any errors and ambiguities I come across, so that if and when the opportunity arises for a further site-visit I can easily spot these on the drawings. Any second 'bites' at measuring I then add to the drawing in a second, easily identifiable colour. Quite often in addition I make a separate check-off list of omissions. It is bad enough to have to return to site to correct one's errors (though better than guessing); to come back a second time with incomplete information is extremely exasperating.

d Tapes and rules
No one measuring rule is really adequate to perform all the measuring functions you will need. Depending on the size of the building and on the number of assistants you can call upon to measure it, both rigid and flexible rules will be needed. If you are surveying on your own, a folding rod is the most useful instrument, although a builder's spring steel tape, 2 metres long, will do for measuring short lengths, expecially if it is of the type provided with a lock to prevent the spring returning it to its holder. It is however frustrating to try and use one of these at the limit of its length owing to its lack of rigidity.

Because of the inherent danger of error using cumulative dimensions, it is undoubtedly better to take running dimensions with a

100 ft tape. These are obtainable in different materials. Steel tapes are probably more accurate but need more looking after as they rust easily. Fabric tapes need little maintenance beyond the occasional wipe after use in wet weather.

The real difficulty in measuring is that of taking accurate dimensions at high level. I suspect that a large number of measured drawings, however convincingly drawn up, could be demonstrated to become less accurate in proportion to the distance of the element measured above the floor. It is clear that without a ladder, with an ordinary rod you can take accurate vertical dimensions up to about 10 feet from floor level. At that height however, it is impossible to take horizontal dimensions at all. The folding rod with one arm bent at right angles helps out a bit, but in turn reduces the height at which you can measure. I use a home-made ten-foot measuring rod made of a single length of hardwood strip. Feet and inches are marked in contrasting colours – odd feet have inches demarcated in black and white, even in red and green. This extends my radius of action by about five feet. In addition a similarly coloured further arm can be bolted to this to project horizontally from the top to take horizontal dimensions at the limit of height. This is all a bit cumbersome, but it travels on the car roof rack and is a great deal better than guesswork.

e Ladders, scaffolding

Beyond a certain height, any kind of rule becomes unwieldy and in any case impossible to read, so you must have recourse to ladders and scaffolding. With any luck ladders or steps will be available on site, but I do occasionally lug a ladder to the site on my roof-rack. I use an extending ladder of aluminium (lighter than wood) and its extended length broadly coincides with the maximum height at which I am in any case prepared to operate.

It is a very expensive and elaborate matter to make provision for a building to be scaffolded simply so that it can be measured. I have never persuaded anyone that this was worthwhile. It is quite a good idea, on the other hand, to keep an eye open to see when buildings that deserve to be recorded have scaffolding erected for maintenance or other purposes, and to take the opportunity (which may not recur for a long time) to make a measured survey. It will not usually be difficult to get permission to do this, though problems of insurance may have to be overcome. Measuring buildings from scaffolding is a luxury compared with cavorting on ladders.

f Special equipment

Although most ordinary measuring jobs can be carried out with the very simple equipment so far discussed, for some more exacting tasks more sophisticated equipment will be needed. The problem of measuring lofty buildings has already been touched on; to overcome this, binoculars are often very useful for two distinct purposes. First, where a building is constructed of regularly coursed materials – brick walls, shingled spires – the counting of courses gives good evidence of dimensions. Binoculars are of help in course-counting, particularly where very high buildings, chimney stacks and so forth are involved. Second, when measuring a high building or a tower, a flexible tape can often be dropped down the length of the wall from the parapet or an upper window. It is surprisingly difficult to read off the dimensions on the tape with the naked eye, above about fifteen feet, not because the gradations cannot be seen but because the figures are indistinguishable. Binoculars are invaluable for this, especially if you are attempting to establish heights in this manner on anything but a very calm day, as any slight breeze makes the tape vibrate in a manner not conducive to accuracy.

In the Grand Fleet in the old days, the ships when at sea were required to keep very precisely to the distances ordered for them. To this end the midshipman of the watch spent most of his time 'station keeping'. Armed with a sextant he would repeatedly check the angle between the waterline and masthead of the battleship next ahead. Knowing the ship's masthead height, from the sextant angle the distance could be determined, and the ship's speed adjusted as necessary to maintain station. Nautical Tables (for astronomical navigation) generally contain a 'Table of Masthead Angles' (fig. 1).

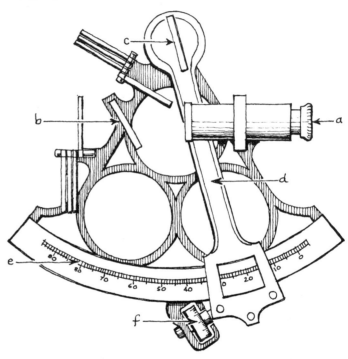

Fig 1 Operation of the sextant.
a *Viewing telescope.*
b *Glass screen, half clear, half silvered.*
c *Mirror, mounted on*
d *Swinging arm.*
e *Scale in degrees.*
f *Vernier scale and clutch, to engage swinging arm with scale.*

If you are lucky enough to have access to a sextant, you can use this principle in reverse to obtain very accurate dimensions of, for example, the height of church spires. The operation of the sextant is fairly apparent from inspection. You look through the eye-piece at a glass screen. Half of this is clear and you can see through it. The other half is silvered and reflects the view from a second mirror or prism mounted on a swinging arm. To measure the angle between, say, weathercock and ground, align the arm so that the weathercock, seen in the mirror half, coincides with the ground level seen in the plain half. Read off the result from the curved scale. This will give you an angle accurate to 0.1 of a minute of arc. The accuracy of the height measured will thus be high, provided you can establish with accuracy your horizontal distance from the object. This can either be done by direct measurement, or, provided you have an accurate plan survey, by adapting another navigational device, the three-point 'fix', again using the sextant or a traversing theodolite, to take horizontal angles. The trigonometry of this height calculation is not complicated; height = horizontal distance × tan θ,

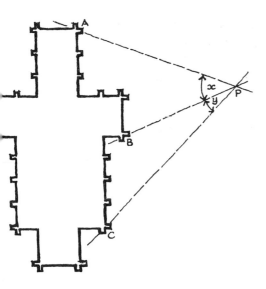

Fig 2 Position plotting using the sextant. Horizontal as well as vertical angles can be measured with the sextant. For example, angles x and y plotted on an overlay to give lines AP, BP and CP, produce a unique location for P.

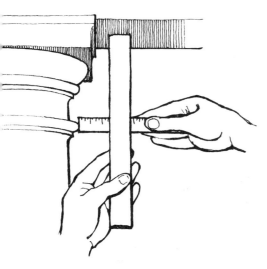

Fig 3 Measuring profiles: using rule and straightedge.
Both the rule and the straightedge must have true square ends, and the rule must be graduated from its end.

Fig 4 Measuring profiles: using adjustable comb.
The comb consists of a series of parallel steel spines sliding in a steel carriage. Superior versions have locking devices to fix the spines once they have taken up the profile of the moulding against which they are pressed.

where θ is the sextant angle measured. (Nautical Tables are no good to the architectural draughtsman, because they are based on the assumption that you are standing on the bridge of a super-Dreadnought rather than flat on the ground) (fig. 2).

So much for the sextant. An instrument more familiar to architects which also measures angles is the theodolite. This again is rather a specialised piece of equipment, but indispensable if you have to set out an accurate datum line to measure heights, particularly if the building you are measuring is both big and distorted. In his book on architectural drawing, Spiers describes a survey of St Albans Cathedral undertaken in 1879 by James Neale, who established an East–West datum line through the north door of the screen using a theodolite, in order to measure the differential settlement of the building. (He used the same line to measure offsets to establish the plan, with the aid of a 16-foot set square!) This is measuring on a grand scale – the nave alone is some 284 feet long – and a somewhat daunting and solemn task, but the establishment of a horizontal datum line either by a stretched line, flags or chalk marks on walls, or whatever, is an essential preliminary in measuring a building affected by differential settlement.

If you do not have access to a theodolite to set up this datum, a bricklayer's spirit level can be used with some accuracy, especially in conjunction with a long straightedge. This useful tool also contains a second level to allow accurate verticals to be set up, and this also will be helpful on occasion (plate 31).

The other aspect of measuring which frequently calls for specialised equipment is the taking of profiles of mouldings. You can do this with a fair degree of success with two rigid rules, one across the face of the moulding to form a datum, the other used to take offsets from it. This method, admirable for large or coarse mouldings, will hardly do for the architrave of a door. Traditionally this finer work was captured with the aid of a flexible strip of lead or copper, which was modelled to the profile of the moulding, carefully withdrawn and traced. A pleasing alternative is the adjustable comb. This consists of a series of long plates or steel needles gripped in a holder so that they lie parallel to one another but can slide to and fro. The comb is simply pressed against the moulding so that it takes up its shape, which is then traced off (figs. 3 and 4).

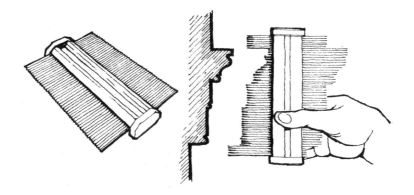

3 Site surveying   Measured drawing is divided into two separate processes, surveying the building on the site, and translating the survey drawings and notes into finished drawings in the office. The site survey itself can be conducted in one of two ways, which I will call, for the sake of identification, scale and freehand plotting. In essence, scale plotting consists of building up properly measured drawings on the site, while freehand plotting consists of making freehand sketches and annotating them with dimensions and notes for later translation.

Each method has its advantages and disadvantages; moreover there is no reason why the two different techniques should not be used to record different components of the same survey.

a Scale plotting   Scale plotting, the execution of preliminary measured drawings on the site, is generally advocated as the ideal method of producing measured drawings. Spiers makes 'measure and plot on the spot' an inflexible rule. This method undoubtedly makes for the greatest accuracy, since, as the dimensions are plotted one by one as they are taken, any errors are at once detected, and can be corrected at once. Furthermore, it is impossible to overlook a dimension, since all must be taken if the drawing is to be completed. It reduces the need for ability in freehand drawing, whilst making it easier for the expert freehand draughtsman to insert freely-drawn detail within a measured framework. Accuracy of scale and proportion of bas-relief carvings, capitals and other details is thus easy to achieve (plate 32).

On the other hand, scale plotting is a somewhat slow and ponderous procedure. You must carry a proper drawing board and tee-square to the site and unless you are prepared to carry it about the site with you, you must find somewhere light, dry and out of the wind to set it up. Once you have set up camp you will have to keep returning to it with fresh information. It is a process more suited to the solo draughtsman than to the measuring team, since the slow speed will waste a good deal of their time, but measuring with a team allows running dimensions to be taken and is therefore preferable. A modified form of scale plotting is to use a scale but not a square, on a detail paper pad with an inserted grid as previously described. This gives a sufficient degree of accuracy to allow the proper drawing of freehand detail, and allows for the checking of the work as it proceeds, without rendering you immobile. This modified method I use to a considerable extent for making detail drawings of orders, monuments and other details. I find it especially suitable for large-scale work, such as full-size details. In cases where there is no likelihood of a second site visit, some degree of scale plotting is desirable, as it is all too easy otherwise to return to the office and find that your site notes lack the one ruling dimension you need to start an accurate transcription. It is important to annotate scaled surveys with all the dimensions taken, for on return to your drawing office you will generally want to re-draw, rather than simply trace them.

b Freehand plotting   Freehand plotting has almost exactly the opposite advantages and disadvantages. It needs the minimum equipment and the minimum fuss. It can be carried out rapidly, kept very simple or elaborated as far as required. Once the survey has been drawn out, the work of adding dimensions, with assistants to hold the tape, can be carried on at great speed with the least waste of their time. Freehand plotting can save time in another way. It allows you to be very selective in what you measure, and to avoid repetition. If a church aisle has six identical windows it is seldom necessary to measure more than one in detail. In fact, provided the leading dimensions are properly established, it is pointless to measure more than one half of one window in detail. Repetition should always be avoided, since economy of effort at the survey stage means less risk of lapses of concentration, which are fatal to good measured work. This said, one must beware of local variations in apparently identical details. Movement and distortion through great age needs to be recorded, as much as does the variation in carving from capital to capital in a nineteenth-century church.

Considerable accuracy is needed in the initial freehand sketch. Again, the reference grid behind detail paper is a great help in achieving rectangularity, or you may wish to go so far as to measure and plot a reference grid showing, say, the bay-spacing of a regular plan, before filling in the detail freehand. It is important to try to produce a neat, consistent sketch before you start annotating. Again, mistakes in dimensioning cannot readily be detected, although some obvious ones can be amended at the drawing-up stage. Likewise, the omission of vital dimensions is much easier than it sounds, which is why it is a good idea to measure all four walls of a room even if it seems absolutely rectangular. I find it easy to neglect internal and external wall-thicknesses, and floor thicknesses on section, and it is often extremely difficult to deduce these later. Besides, a degree of duplication of dimensions gives a very good opportunity for later cross-checking of accuracy, and any dimensions which are omitted deny you this worthwhile facility. In general then, freehand plotting is much easier – I should think the vast majority of surveys measured for alteration jobs are done in this way – but it is comforting to be in a position to return to the site for a second visit later if necessary (plates 33 and 34).

c Organisation of the work

To carry out a successful measured survey, it is as well to be methodical over the planning of the job. The starting point is the purpose of the survey. The type and number of drawings you require for a complete visual record will be quite different from the drawings needed for the design of a small rear extension to a building. Again, the scope of the drawings is to some extent determined by the time actually available to carry them out, as well as by the number of assistants you can muster. Speed of working is a very individual matter, and only experience will teach you roughly how much you can get done in a given time. I generally work fairly fast, and reckon that I can probably draw plans, front and rear elevations and a section of an average London house, and with one (preferably two) assistants, dimension these drawings in a fairly long day's work.

This rate of work does rather depend on my mood at the time, and I find that however fast I can in theory work, in practice there is a limit to the length of time for which I can concentrate. In this respect I find, when plotting freehand, that plans are less demanding than elevations, and sections are worst of all. Details I find very difficult to concentrate on for more than about an hour, although I enjoy drawing them. If your concentration varies in this way with the nature of the task you might find it helpful to vary the tasks themselves, interspersing the plotting of plans and elevations for example. Adding the dimensions to a freehand plot is perhaps less demanding; provided you have prepared drawings of sufficient accuracy the addition of dimensions takes on a refreshing logic, like writing in the answers on a crossword puzzle which is easier than the one you usually solve. At the same time the accuracy of the dimensions must be watched with some care, especially if you are employing an assistant to read them off the tape for you to note down – remember that your assistant is subconsciously less concerned with accuracy than you are, for he does not have the subsequent task of making sense of them. Choose your measuring assistants carefully. It is surprising how many cannot read a tape with any consistent degree of accuracy at all.

The scales you choose for your on-site drawings depend primarily on the need for clarity, and on whether you have chosen to measure the building by scale plotting or freehand plotting. In neither case is it essential for the scales to correspond with those you envisage for the finished work, and indeed, if you are plotting freehand you will not normally be working closely to a scale. Some correspondence of preliminary and final scales may however be of assistance when scale plotting. The drawings can be used as an easy method of comparison when the finished work is being prepared, thus giving immediate warning of error in transcription. Moreover, it may be a help to know the compass of the drawings when working out the size and composition of the finished sheets.

What is more important, whichever mode of plotting you employ, is that the scale of the drawings should not be too small, since all the drawings have to be annotated with dimensions, and the more cramped these are, the greater the risk of ambiguity and error. I believe that 1:100 is just too small a scale to dimension adequately, and that for most scale plotting jobs a scale of 1:50 is best. Drawing freehand you can afford to draw a little, (but not much) smaller than 1:50. This immediately brings you into the difficulty of fitting the plot onto a single sheet, but provided the break-points in a plan are clearly marked, I think it is better to let the plan spill over onto a number of separate sheets, rather than risk lack of clarity in dimensions. If the building you are faced with is of any size, it will probably contain a good deal of repetition in form, In this case it is best to start by measuring the framework of principal dimensions, plotted to quite small scale, say 1:200, and then to make separate drawings of components (fig. 5, plate 35).

Mention of scale raises the question of whether measured drawings should be produced in metric or imperial scales. I have tended to shy away from metric scales for measured drawings. Most of the buildings you measure were constructed in imperial measure, and this determines the 'grain' of their ruling dimensions. The setting out of brickwork on plan in multiples of nine inches is a common example, and window and door sizes may well be rounded out to the nearest three or four inches. This dimensional logic running through a building is easier to detect if you measure in imperial, and certainly if the drawings are wholly for record purposes, I see no reason to depart from imperial measure. When you are conducting a measured survey with a view to altering the building, however, it may make for great inconvenience if the drawings are to imperial scales, since you will almost certainly design the new work in metric. I have come to the conclusion that the proper solution is to measure imperial, but plot to metric using a conversion scale. The imposition of metric work onto imperial which you propose in the building works is thus exactly mirrored in the production of the survey and design drawings.

If you are measuring by freehand plotting, there is no point in your assistants accompanying you to the site in the first instance. There is nothing for them to do until you have produced the sketch drawings for the whole team to dimension. You should arrange therefore, a long enough solo session in the building before they arrive. Leave yourself plenty of time for this, or you may find their premature presence leads you to hurry unduly over the drawings at the expense of accuracy. Professor Brunskill in his book *Vernacular Architecture* gives an admirable 'operation order' of almost military concision for the measuring of a building. One of the points which emerges clearly from this is the need for system in measuring. If you get into the habit of conducting the survey in a systematic manner, you are unlikely to find any serious omissions from the plot. No two systems will be alike. My own sequence of working, once the sketch drawings are done is generally as follows:

i. In each room in turn, measure all four walls, starting from the corner to the left of the entrance door, working clockwise and using running dimensions (as far as the furniture will allow). Note as many wall thicknesses, at doorways and windows, as necessary, and do not omit the depth of chimney breasts and other offsets. Take diagonals where the rectangularity of the building is suspect, and the floor to ceiling height (which I show in a square box to avoid ambiguity). Note dimensions on plan of any changes in floor level; note any ceiling beams, etc.

ii. Measure anti-clockwise round the exterior of the building again using running dimensions as far as possible. In the case of a

Fig 5 Plotting repetitive elements: reference grid. (see also Plate 35). The screen at Kilndown Church has fourteen identical bays apart from the central entrance. The grid establishes the leading dimensions and only one bay (together with any minor variations in detail) need be fully drawn and measured.

CHRIST CHURCH KILNDOWN

Reference grid for chancel screen

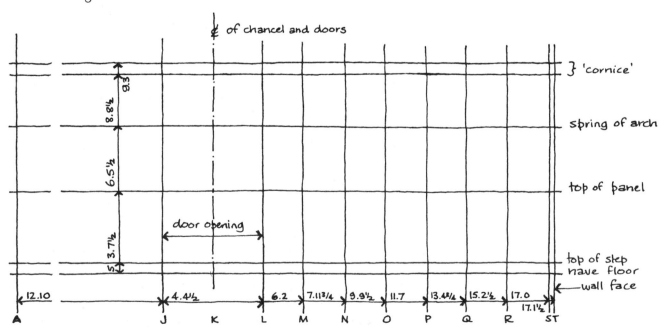

church, this probably means measuring across the face of the buttresses, and going back to measure individual bays. Again, note any offsets, and at as many points as possible, doorways and windows, note datum points where the inside plan can be related to the outside. It is embarrassing later to find you cannot fit one in the other.

iii. Measure such triangulation as will enable you to fix the location of the building within its site, if the disposition of this is known or, vice versa, to establish the overall site dimensions so that the whole site can be drawn round the building. Make a note of any bench mark heights, especially when alterations to drainage are envisaged.

iv. Establish the overall internal height on the section, where possible from running dimensions using a tape dropped down the stairwell. This, coupled with the floor to ceiling heights, and local changes in floor level, will give you floor thicknesses. Measure sill and window head heights in each room, using a datum level related back to the stairwell heights if there is appreciable vertical distortion.

v. Read off vertical dimensions externally, where possible from a tape lowered down the wall face. Again take care to note reference heights at windows, and especially at door thresholds, to relate internal and external dimensions.

Whether your drawing is comprehensible or not will depend on how meticulous you are in dimensioning and annotating. There is some danger of confusing the lines of the actual drawing with dimension lines, so the latter should be put in very lightly, cross-marked at the positions where dimensions are taken, and further ticked or arrowed to show whether or not the dimension noted is part of a running sequence. The actual dimensions should be inserted as small and as neatly as possible. It is amazing how easy it is to run out of space for notes on a part of a drawing. All this is easier to preach than to practise, but it is worth making some effort over. You will evolve your own method of annotation. I show my own merely as an example – arrow heads for the ends of dimension sequences, diagonal marks for intermediate measurements. I also generally omit the dimension line itself, except for diagonals (figs. 6 and 7).

The sequence of operations described applies, with some minor modification, to scale plotting as well as to freehand work. You need rather less time on site without your assistants, since the method depends on the direct transcription of dimensions taken onto the drawing. Where the building is of any great size or complexity, it will probably be easier to make small freehand plots of individual sections, and then transfer them to the main plot. However you organise it, it is difficult to avoid periods of idleness for your helpers. It is probably better if possible for this kind of survey to be conducted by two people both expert at the work, so that while one is drawing up plans, for example, the other can concentrate on details.

For detail drawing, assistants are generally superfluous, except to hold the foot of the ladder when you are working at high level. For doors and windows, tracery and so forth, a proper third angle projection can be drawn, on a sketch grid, showing the detail in plan, elevation and section (plate 36). This way you ensure that the measuring is tackled methodically and that you leave nothing out. Surface decoration, bas-reliefs and, indeed, any detail of which you propose only to draw the elevation, can be drawn out, preferably by scale plotting, in planar form. When undertaking this kind of detail, especially when it involves a good deal of freehand work, I take co-ordinates of salient points, plot them and 'join the dots'. A high degree of dimensional accuracy is normally only necessary in order to capture the proportion of the thing, without which its essential characteristics cannot be recorded (plate 37).

Often, in measuring elevations, you may find it convenient to produce plots to three different scales. First a drawing of the entire elevation, avoiding detail and showing the leading dimensions of the whole; second, a general drawing of the individual elements; third, details of tracery, windows, doors and other details. One point about line drawing showing leading dimensions: although I

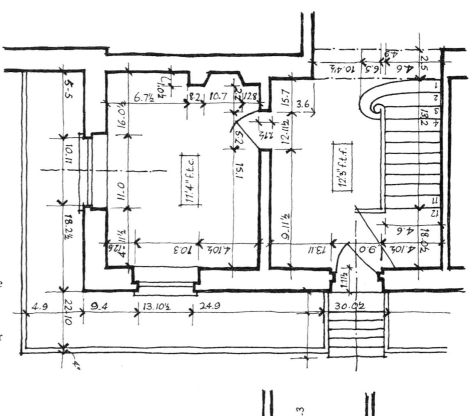

Fig 6 Plotting dimensions using dimension lines.
Part ground floor plan of a house. The dimension lines are kept as light as possible so as not to confuse the plan. Arrows indicate running dimensions. Figures in boxes indicate floor-to-floor and floor-to-ceiling dimensions.

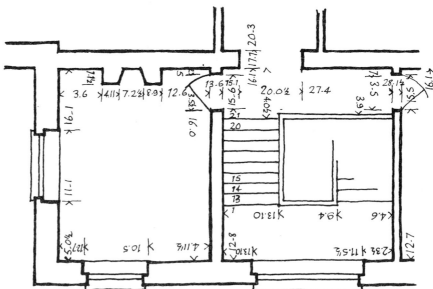

Fig 7 Plotting dimensions without dimension lines. Part upper floor plan corresponding with fig 6. Provided the plan is not too complex no ambiguity arises from the omission of the dimension lines. Arrows again indicate running dimensions.

25

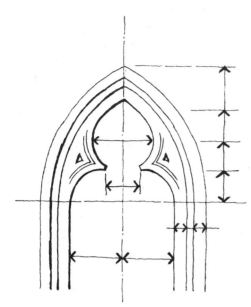

Fig 8 Measuring tracery.
The minimum dimensions needed are indicated by the arrowheads. The radii of various components can be determined by the same means as shown in Fig 8 for determining radii of arches.

almost automatically put in centre-lines of bays, etc. on drawings of this kind, it is as well to remember that these cannot actually be measured directly on site.

It is repeatedly necessary when measuring elevations to establish the setting-out centres of arches, both circular and pointed. The diagram (fig. 9) shows the essential measurements. It is important to determine the spring of the arch and measure the clear span, and the height of the apex or crown above the springing-line. I quite often, especially when measuring an open arcade, stretch a line across the spring of the arch in order to provide an exact datum for the height. Similarly, the form of cusped tracery can be determined with accuracy if the co-ordinates of the cusps, and the widest points of the adjoining arcs together with their diameters are all measured – often quite a laborious business but one where too much short-cutting leads to subsequent frustration when setting out (fig. 8).

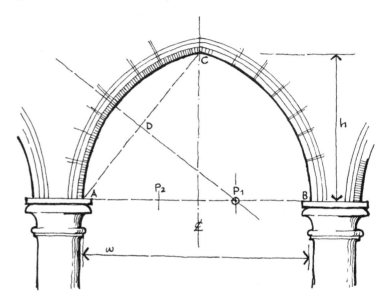

Fig 9 Measuring arches.
Measure the width w and height h. Draw points A B and C and bisect AC at D with line at right angles. Where this cuts AB at P1 is the centre of the arc AC.

4 Estimating dimensions

All sorts of methods, both crude and sophisticated, are available for estimating dimensions. These are useful at various stages of the work. In the first instance, it is useful to have a fairly good idea of the main dimensions of a building to facilitate setting out the first plot, whether freehand or scale. All sorts of familiar objects can be used to assess large dimensions. For example, the sportsman's cricket pitch (at 22 yards) is broadly equivalent to the railway enthusiast's coach (60 – 65 feet). Experience will enable you to build up your own individual estimating scale of this kind. Coming to the more accurate assessment of somewhat shorter lengths, most people can pace a yard with fair accuracy, and if you take a size 10 in shoes your shoes are almost exactly one foot long – a useful variation of Sir Reginald's umbrella.

Just as these stratagems are useful to refine your guesses about measurements on plan, so can a number of dodges be used to estimate heights. Your own height is the first useful guide; better still, use your assistant as a vertical measuring rod. Experience gives a good idea of likely domestic room heights. Door and window head heights vary sufficiently to be misleading, but it is quite easy to measure the door height and estimate its proportion of the total height of a room. Heights can sometimes be assessed from photographs, but beware of foreshortening which distorts vertical dimensions on photographs to a significant extent.

When you come to the actual measuring process, more accurate means of estimation can be of help. In cases where direct measuring is impossible, such as spires, tall buildings and chimney stacks, some kind of estimation is essential. In these circumstances, happy is the draughtsman whose building is made of brick. Brickwork is generally built up with great dimensional consistency, thus providing its own built-in vertical scale. It is common in the south east of England for brickwork to rise by four courses to the foot – in the Midlands bricks are somewhat thicker and four courses to $13\frac{1}{2}$ inches may be closer to the mark – but in each case check by measuring up to 20 courses to establish the scale. Then you can simply count the number of courses, from a selected datum, to establish the height of sills, window heads, band courses, eaves and chimney stack details. I generally try again to use 'running dimensions', although the counting of courses on a tall building is a somewhat dizzying affair. Brick dimensions can also be used to establish horizontal measurements, but here their accuracy is less reliable. Again, you should measure a number of bricks and half-bricks in a course (depending on the bond) to set up the scale, but beware of cut bricks used to make up 'non-modular' dimensions, and variations in the thickness of mortar perpends.

Regularly coursed ashlar may be almost as good a dimensional indicator as brickwork, but there is often a deliberate variation in course depth to allow stones of different sizes to be worked into a wall, or even to achieve a deliberate visual foreshortening. However, you may be able to piece together a vertical scale which will give you good estimates of the height of elements of the elevation which are inaccessible. Similarly, stucco work is often scribed with horizontal and vertical joints to simulate stone, but here the variations in depth of course, made at the whim of the plasterer usually to align with features such as window sills and heads, are more difficult to spot at a glance, and rigorous measuring is required which may obviate the value of the scribing as a height indicator. Tile hanging (usually $4–4\frac{1}{2}$ inch gauge) and weatherboard (clapboard) are two other finishes with obvious potential as height-gauges.

When you come to the estimation of greater heights, and where no clue can be obtained from the coursing of the material, other means must be found. I have touched earlier on the use of the sextant, but heights can be estimated quite accurately without recourse to such sophisticated instruments. Two methods are commonly employed, both involving the use of similar triangles, and both confined to level sites if a high degree of precision is sought.

Both methods are best explained diagramatically. In the first, a pole of known length is set up vertically and the position found where, adopting an undignified posture prone upon the ground, the top of the pole coincides with the element whose height is to be determined (fig. 10). The distance of the pole and the observer from the building being measured, the height can be determined. Alternatively, the length of shadow cast on the ground by the pole and by the object to be measured can both be marked simultaneously, and the height determined geometrically, (similar triangles) (fig. 11). This method is the less accurate of the two, owing to the

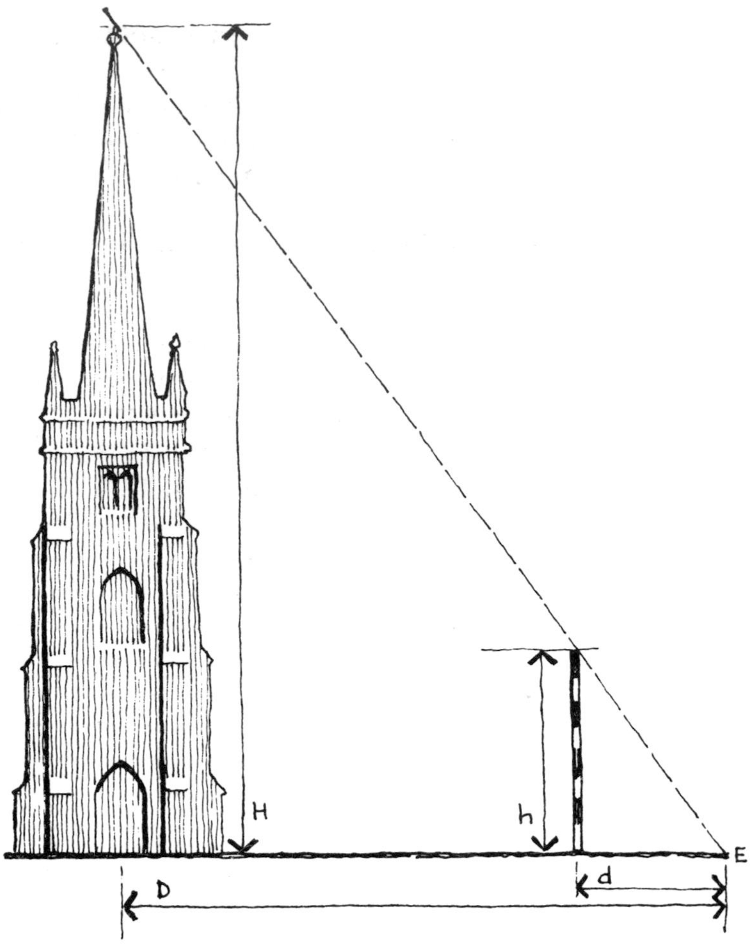

Fig 10 Estimating height: comparison
with staff of known height.
As can be seen this is an undignified
business, as the observer's eye has to be
at point E for the dimensions indicated
to be obtained.

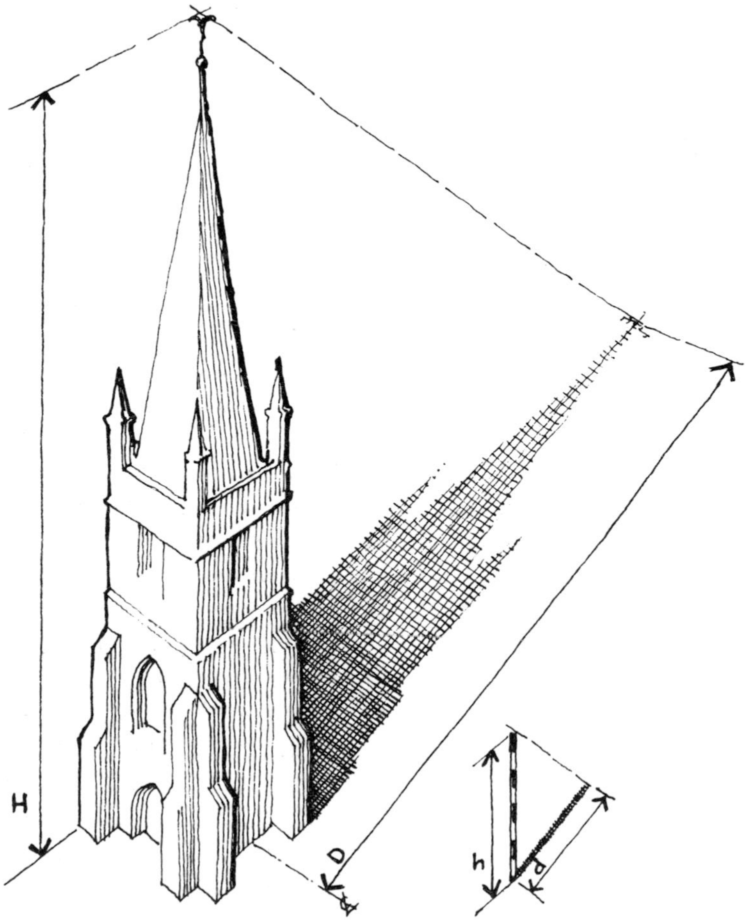

Fig 11 Estimating height: comparison of
shadow-lengths.
A variation of the method indicated in
Fig 10, again using the principle of
similar triangles.

28

blurring of the shadow of an object of any height. In both cases the longer the pole the better, and in both cases the verticality of the pole is essential to accuracy. These methods give reasonable estimation of heights, and are particularly useful as a check on other means.

5 Supporting information   Although in theory, a survey carefully plotted and dimensioned on site should provide all the information you need to produce complete measured drawings, very often additional information will be of help. Not only will local variations be easier to record by other means but ambiguities which do not become apparent at the time can be more easily ironed out in the office if supplementary information is available. The most obvious means of providing this is by photography, and hardly any thorough survey is carried out without augmenting the measured work with photographs.

You do not need to be an expert photographer to take adequate photographs for this purpose, although it is worth taking some trouble if the results are to be of value in supplementing the finished drawings for the benefit of others, rather than simply being useful as notes for the draughtsman alone. Choice of camera is not critical. Some people use Polaroid or similar 'instant' cameras, which do have the advantages that you know immediately what you have taken, and can take further pictures to make good any deficiencies. For years I used an antiquated Kodak, size 116, a somewhat ponderous moving-bellows camera only one generation on, I should think, from the brass-and-mahogany era. This had the advantage that the prints developed straight from the negatives, without enlargement, were large enough for most measured drawing use. When film became unobtainable in 116 size I switched to using an inexpensive 35 mm. camera, but few straightforward measuring jobs require as many as 24 photos, so I now normally use a Rolleicord twin-lens camera from which I get twelve $2\frac{1}{4}$ inch square photos. The prints are usually enlarged, but I suppose the parsimonious could use direct prints from negatives of this size, and count brick courses from them with a magnifying glass.

For interiors, a tripod is, if not absolutely essential, a great deal better than a pile of hymn-books. Lighting levels are often very low in the interiors one finds oneself measuring, and very long exposures with the aperture stopped well down produce the best effect. Outside, long exposures with small apertures are again preferable to short exposures with wide apertures, particularly if depth of focus is required. It is better to photograph outside when the sun is obscured by cloud if information rather than artistic affect is what you want, to avoid strong contrast and impenetrable shadows.

Apart from photographs, all sorts of annotations help in the deciphering and transcription of on-site drawings. Notes on materials and colours are particularly important as it is easy to be confused by these once you are away from the site. Perspective sketches of details which are at all ambiguous on elevation or plan, and sketches of items worthy of note in themselves are worth taking, even if these may not appear in detail in the finished drawings. Notes of dates of origin, attributions to architects and builders and so forth should be copied from foundation stones and commemorative plaques.

Do not overlook as a further valuable source of information any drawings of the building which may already exist. Local authority Building Regulation departments, local builders and architects may well have drawings if the building has been recently altered, although they have some difficulty unearthing them. Even if you are so suspicious of such drawings as to wish to re-measure entirely, they serve as an excellent basis for setting out your initial plot, which can be done with some certainty in the comfort of your office before you proceed to the site.

6 Full-size measuring grids

I have referred to the drawing of details by measuring the co-ordinates and 'joining the dots'. Where a detail of this kind is very extensive, this method may lead to error simply because of the difficulty of judging the rectangularity of the co-ordinates. This difficulty is exacerbated in cases where the object to be measured is not itself rectangular in overall shape. Highly decorated ceilings, large scale bas-reliefs and enriched wall panels are instances. In such cases I find it best to set up a full-size measuring grid over the object to be measured, dividing it into squares of manageable size. Reference to a specific example best illustrates the method. Following a fire in a seventeenth century house in the City of London it was desired to restore the elaborate *stucco duro* ceilings. Parts of them had collapsed, and it was decided to measure what was left, and build up complete measured drawings with reference to photographs of the ceilings as they existed before the fire.

To do this, a grid of string was pinned up over the ceilings, the strings one foot apart stretched between light pins driven into the plain plaster. The diagonals were also set out and measured, since none of the ceilings was precisely rectangular. Each square of the grid was drawn separately, in this instance full size, and the whole of the surviving ceiling decoration was thus recorded. This information was then translated onto measured drawings drawn to a scale of $1\frac{1}{2}$ in.:1 foot. To fill in the details of the fallen sections of the ceilings, a matching grid was overlaid on the earlier photographs (plates 38–41).

Not only does this kind of grid make for greater precision in measuring co-ordinates, but the division of the surface into squares each of which can be worked on separately concentrates the mind on each square individually and, I think, makes the whole task seem less daunting.

7 Labelling drawings

It may seem like a truism, but it is of paramount importance to label site-drawings adequately. It is all too easy, particularly if drawing up the survey has to be postponed, for confusion to arise over which drawing is which. This is especially true where a number of details are produced to supplement a basic elevation. Details of doors and windows demonstrating local variations in design are very easily confused.

All site drawings should at least be annotated with the following:
Name or address of building
Description of drawing: 'first floor plan' etc.
Date of execution
Scale (in the case of scale plotting).
Where the work is of any complexity it is as well to number each drawing in turn. Any detail drawings appertaining to the main

drawing can be given suffix numbers, the location of details being indicated by a ringed number. Where full size or other grids are established these are identified (for example letters horizontally, figures vertically), so that details can be related unambiguously to the grid.

8 Safety   I do not think the subject of site-work is complete without brief mention of safety. It is taken for granted that no question of personal risk arises from the surveying of buildings, but if too casual an attitude is adopted it can prove to be a dangerous occupation in more than one way. However, no risk need arise provided some elementary precautions are observed. For the most part it is enough to keep an observant eye on suspended floors, especially in derelict buildings, and to avoid loose or rotted floorboards. Often the condition of an upper floor can be assessed from the room below. If a floor is so deteriorated that you feel constrained to walk near the periphery of the room, it is probably unwise to walk on it at all. Always carry a torch when measuring interiors – I should not wish to repeat the eerie and disorientating experience of walking in a totally unlit room so badly affected by dry-rot that the boards gave way with each successive step!

Do not attempt to defy the laws of gravity, when making use of ledges and sills above ground level, to take details of window tracery or cornices. On ladders do not attempt to extend your radius of action beyond a reasonable limit, and station an assistant to keep the foot from sliding.

Above all, and particularly if you embark on recording an unoccupied building by yourself, let someone know where you are going, and the probable duration of your visit. To be incarcerated alone in a belfry by a jammed trap door is just as exasperating, and potentially as dangerous as falling down the belfry stairs. Finally, it is wise before carrying out any but the most routine measuring work, to make sure that your insurance (or that of your employer on your behalf) provides cover for such activities.

IV DRAWING UP SURVEYS

The best way of drawing is from the top downwards to preserve the cleanness of the paper. Sir Roger Pratt; from a notebook of c. 1660.

1 Equipment

Just as the provision of proper equipment is necessary to the conduct of the site survey, so it is essential to provide yourself with the means to translate the survey into adequate measured drawings. For the most part, of course, the equipment needed is the same as that provided for everyday use in the drawing office, no additional expense of any significance being called for provided the office is properly set up. Not that too much should be made of this business of equipment. Styles of working vary widely and personal preference is all-important. I do find that as I get older I look for higher standards of comfort and convenience, and I think I can claim some advance in accuracy since the days when I embarked on the production of measured drawings without even a tee-square. What is important in the choice of equipment is that the things that you use should function accurately and smoothly, so that you do not have to dissipate nervous energy and concentration on making them work, but can devote your entire attention to the actual business of drawing.

a Drawing boards and drawing stations

Choice of drawing board size and type depends on how much space you have available as well as on how seriously you are to pursue the craft of measured drawing. Doing most of my drawings at home, I am a somewhat peripatetic draughtsman, choosing my workplace according to whether I desire warmth, company, daylight, musical accompaniment and so on. I use several portable boards including an old 'double-elephant' (42 in. × 32 in., 1067 mm. × 813 mm.) of rather superior construction with an ebony edge, and an 'imperial' (32 in. × 23 in., 813 mm. × 585 mm.) which is easier to carry about the house. Either of these I prop up on any convenient table on an offcut of four-by-two. For lengthy and more serious work I use a properly planned drawing station (fig. 12), the central item of which is an AO drawing board (50 in. × 36 in., 1270 mm. × 920 mm.) mounted on a metal stand and fitted with a simple parallel motion. My board is adustable for rake only. If you are investing in a board of this kind I should advise spending the extra money on a stand adjustable for both rake and height.
I like to keep all my boards prepared in the same way, with a clear acetate sheet stretched over a backing of feint-ruled graph-paper. The acetate accepts draughting tape without rapid deterioration, and the graph-paper grid is useful both for establishing the size and layout of drawings and setting up sheets square on the board, and for adding lettering to drawings without having to rule guidelines.
Essential to the drawing station is as much flat work-top surface as possible. I use the tops of adjoining cupboards, and 'overspill' onto

the nearby dining table. Storage is also important, and having insufficient space to accommodate a plan-chest, I keep drawings rolled up in cut lengths of pvc downpipe built into some deep shelving. Incidentally, tracings should always be rolled drawing-side out, so that they will be flat when they are subsequently unrolled. My drawing station is completed by a generous amount of small shelving for the general impedimenta of draughtsmanship, and of a hessian-over-insulation board lining to the wall behind the board, to produce a large area for pinning up drawings.

Good lighting is of the utmost importance. I obtain general lighting from a single, shaded 3 foot 40 watt fluorescent tube at high level, supplemented by concealed tungsten lamps above the shelves, which by providing cross-lighting help to reduce unwanted shadows. For close illumination my articulated lamp is mounted on the wall so as to be out of the way.

b Choice of materials

Like the site survey, the manner of preparation in the office of measured drawings is governed by their purpose. As I have said, measured drawings are commonly produced either to provide a permanent record, or as a preliminary to alteration, or for the training of students. These separate functions may of course overlap, but each category of use demands slightly different characteristics. These in turn determine the decisions which have to be made before the work of transcribing the site survey is begun, regarding the size of sheets, the scale of the drawings thereon, the type of surface of sheets and the drawing medium. The following need to be taken into account when making these decisions.

For record drawings, the stability of the sheet must be considered. The material must be durable and it must be dimensionally stable, resistant to change in size resulting from changes in temperature or humidity. The drawing method should be capable of clear reproduction by normal professional printing methods, and the sheet size if possible selected with the system of filing in mind. All drawings should carry a drawn scale in case of subsequent dimensional change in the material.

Measured drawings made prior to the alteration of buildings are generally rather more ephemeral; although the opportunity to expand them to serve as record drawings should not be missed as often as it is. Speed of preparation and ease of reproduction by methods normally available to the ordinary drawing office are of importance, and the selection of materials and scales usually corresponds with those of the subsequent design and working drawings. Drawings whose primary purpose is for student training offer more scope for variety of method. Their preparation affords the occasion to introduce students to a wide range of skills, and to experiment with the whole arsenal of drawing materials. It is worth encouraging them, for example, to experience the discipline of pencil drawing on cartridge, and pencil and wash on hot-pressed paper. The opportunity should be taken to forgo the facility of transfer lettering for hand-lettering, and to become familiar with the range of scales, both imperial and metric, available for the expression of architectural design.

Two desirable characteristics remain common to all kinds of measured drawings, accuracy and clarity, whatever media are employed for whatever purpose.

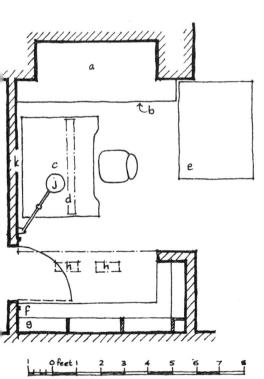

Fig 12 Layout of drawing station.
a Worktop with cupboards under.
b Drawing storage in pvc pipes.
c AO drawing board.
d Fluorescent lamp over board.
e Table.
f Shelf with cupboards under.
g Bookshelves.
h Lamps in soffit of storage space overhead.
j Adjustable lamp.
k Wall surface with hessian on softboard.

c Papers and other surfaces

The vast majority of drawings executed in architects' offices are done on tracing paper of one kind or another. Tracing paper offers, at reasonable cost, two enormous advantages. Obviously, the first is that information can readily be transferred from one sheet to another. This means that the laborious and not always tidy process of setting out a measured survey can be carried out in rough form without having to worry overmuch about finished appearance, and a final tracing subsequently made omitting all the notes, construction lines and other ambiguities which inevitably creep into the first drawing. In addition, in the initial setting out no attention need be paid to the precise layout of the finished sheet, provided the rough sheet will actually accommodate the drawing – and it is surprising how often it doesn't! Tracing paper has, moreover, obvious advantages when it comes to setting up elevations from sections, drawings which are symmetrical but handed or reversed, repetitious elements and so forth. The second major advantage is that tracing can be easily reproduced by dyelines, 'true-to-scale' printing and photo-copying, as well as by the range of processes associated with the printing of books. Tracing paper suffers from some disadvantages however. In particular it is not normally dimensionally stable, and exhibits quite surprising changes of dimensions when the temperature and humidity are varied. This can cause at best irritation, and at the worst, severe loss of accuracy. It is provoking, having carefully set up a plan and begun the final tracing, to return to the board after an overnight break and find that the main lines of the two no longer coincide. To this problem there is no easy solution. It is probably a help not to use tracing paper straight off the roll, but if you have time, to allow the sheet to lie on your drawing board some time before you begin to draw. Another aid to accuracy, albeit apparently extravagant, is to leave your desk lamp burning continuously over the board on which a tracing is set up, to give a degree of control of temperature and humidity (but not so close as to cause local distortion of the paper). It obviously helps too to complete a tracing in as few separate sessions as possible, so rapid draughtsmanship in long spells is to be aimed at.

In the long term, tracing paper is easily damaged and may become brittle. Edge-binding helps to protect sheets from tearing, but unless very carefully applied may itself distort the paper. It is not too difficult to erase and correct errors neatly, but here again local distortion is a risk. From this point of view the thicker and heavier the paper chosen the better, simply because there is more material to go at. Some expert draughtsmen contend that tracing paper does not allow the clearest, most consistent ink line, and most tracing papers are subject, on the one hand to the accumulation of grease on the surface impeding continuous lining in ink and, on the other, a slight abrasive quality in the surface causing rapid wear of pens. Certainly the abrasive nature of tracing paper calls for patience and precision in the use of pencil, and hard pencils need to be used which may not give a satisfactory density of line.

In spite of these disadvantages tracing paper is an appropriate vehicle for most kinds of measured drawing, and some shortcomings can be overcome by the use of plastic film rather than paper. This film is much more robust than tracing papers, resistant to tearing and much less prone to dimensional variation. It is however expensive, and may require special ink to be used in pen work.

A wide range of opaque papers is available, but most come within the two categories of cartridge and moulded papers. Choosing cartridge paper is very much a matter of experience and luck. Cheap cartridge is spongy and soft-surfaced, and neither accepts most common drawing media well nor stands up to erasure. Good cartridge paper is suitable for either ink or pencil, though it is difficult to find one which entirely prevents diffusion and spreading of the ink line. Cartridge papers do not generally take water colour washes or other wet treatments kindly. Most wrinkle and stretch. Many cartridges have one surface more highly finished than the other.

The preparation of elaborately rendered drawings using washes is rare in this hectic age, but occasionally they may be justified, even if mainly as an exercise in skill and patience. Fraser Reekie gives details of moulded papers, and explains in detail how they should be stretched before use. I have found it possible to abbreviate his stretching process somewhat by tacking down the paper edges with gummed brown-paper strip (parcel strip) rather than pasting them to the board. Stretching paper is like a kind of purifying ritual, producing such a quality of surface as to demand a high standard of workmanship in the subsequent drawing, with always the outside chance of bathos when the too-well stretched sheet splits, overnight, across the middle.

Bristol Board, Fashion Board and all kinds of mounting board are also useful for measured drawings, having the advantage that they do not stretch, but not all taking a very crisp line and moreover introducing difficulties with correcting errors, especially if you choose a tinted surface. In fact, although it is sometimes tempting to draw on a coloured board, such artifice is generally inappropriate for the production of serious measured drawings. Possibly the most superior board for presentation work, especially if subsequent reduction and reproduction is envisaged, is the plastic-coated type, for example, Collyer and Southey's CS10, which takes a sharp ink line; here again errors are difficult to correct.

In any instance where the dimensional stability of the drawing surface is in doubt, a linear scale should be added to the drawing.

d Drawing media

A wide range of drawing media is available, but for the production of measured drawings the useful range is confined to pen and ink, and pencil, with the possible addition of water-colour wash and felt pens.

(i) Pen and ink

Pen and ink drawing is universally used. Ink line drawing is clear and unambiguous and reproduces well. It is, however, difficult to correct errors tidily, and some skill is needed to introduce graduations of effect and avoid a certain harshness of line and mechanical appearance. If your drawings are to be fully informative, and at the same time more than just a machine-like record, then it is worth trying to introduce some relief by way of varying line thicknesses, and indicating the texture of materials. This is largely a matter of experience and personal preference, but in bringing a drawing to life in this way you not only inspire people to look at it, but can actually make it clearer and easier to comprehend (plate 42.)

Nearly all drawings are executed in black Indian ink, and if you are drawing on tracing paper, or on any vehicle with a view primarily to reproduction, it hardly seems worthwhile indulging in coloured inks, which seem to me to dilute the integrity of the drawing. The only exception to this is the possibility of using, say, a grey or sepia ink for indicating those parts of a drawing which require less emphasis than the main work, for instance for brick courses or the grain in timber (plate 43).

The range of pens available for ink work deserves consideration. No doubt most draughtsmen use stylus pens (Rotring make or similar), but these are simply the latest stage of a series of developments, none of which need be despised. Although I mainly use a stylus of this kind, I find occasion to use most of the following.

The ordinary nib-pen is of limited value. It is difficult to use against a straight-edge without blotting the work, and most dip-pens have no facility for an ink-reservoir. However, the variable thickness of line obtainable by varying the pressure on the nib has occasional applications especially in freehand work, and a small stock of pen-nibs of different sizes is worth having. On occasions, in a hurry, I also use a fountain pen for drawing up; especially on smooth white paper it is a rapid and quite expressive instrument.

All pens from the quill onwards work, I suppose, by capillary action, and the first type of pen in which the thickness of line could be adjusted was the old-fashioned draughtsman's ruling pen. This has a somewhat better reservoir than the simple dip-pen allowing a reasonable length of line. The difficulty is to prevent it clogging, which necessitates opening up the pen and cleaning the surface of the blades, thus losing the line thickness setting. This can be avoided if you keep the pen stuck in a small jar of water 'between lines', but I am not keen on having too many liquids close to my drawing board, for fear of accidents. Difficult though it may be to adjust to a consistent line width, the pen once adjusted produces a sharp, consistent line which is probably cleaner than that produced by any other form of pen. I find it a useful standby, although of more value in other presentation work, and in architectural model-making, than for measured drawings. If you do decide to invest in one, make sure the blades are very thin and pliable. Cheap ruling pens, and compasses likewise, tend to have stubby blades which do not allow you to draw really fine lines.

The next stage of pen-evolution was the reservoir-nib, culminating in the Graphos pen, which has an ample reservoir occupying the entire barrel of the pen, feeding ink through an elaborate channel to a split nib covered by a swivelling blade. This type again is a useful substitute for the stylus, and much cheaper, but it clogs quite easily and is tedious to dismember and clean. The fine nibs are particularly prone to clogging, and have to be kept exactly parallel with the straightedge to produce a decent line (plate 44).

For measured work, therefore, there is nothing in my view better that the modern stylus. No system is perfect, but the advantages of consistent line, ample reservoir and general ease of use outweigh the disadvantages. Stylus pens repay pampering, especially the finest, and I generally find that if I don't clean out the small-sized ones regularly I end up having to buy new ones, which is an extravagant pastime. The best answer is to buy a set complete with a stand which keeps them damp and prevents clogging, but for those of us who started out with only one or two and added gradually to our collection it never seems quite the right moment to indulge in such a substantial outlay. Using the ink produced by the manufacturer, rather than the somewhat denser traditional Indian ink helps to minimise blockages, and keeping the reservoir topped up reduces accidents, for these pens seem mysteriously to bleed when they become nearly empty. The thickness of line of a given stylus may tend to increase with wear, but this is not normally so marked as to cause concern. I am often asked what sizes I use. I generally restrict my choice (partly through economic necessity) to about four sizes: 0.1 for construction lines, brick courses etc, 0.2 or 0.3 for the bulk of the drawing, depending on the scale, 0.4 for thickening section and 'shadow' lines, and 0.6 or 0.8 for occasional emphasis (fig. 13).

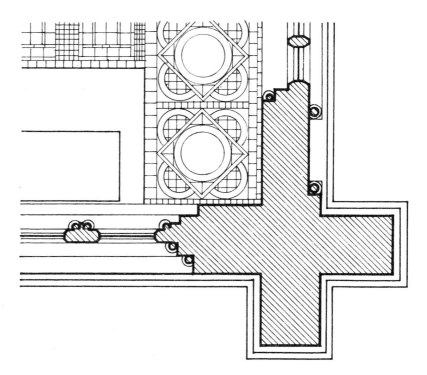

Fig 13 Different stylus widths.
0.1   Floor tiles.
0.15 Hatching to external walls.
0.2   General setting out, window mouldings etc.
0.3   Internal risers and external plinths.
0.4   Main outline of walls.

(ii) Pencil Sir Roger Pratt in the mid-seventeenth century recommended the use of 'Black lead pencils, the blackest and least brittle whereof are the best . . .' He was drawing on 'the most smooth and fine and white parchment or vellum'; in the present day, the choice of pencil will be dictated by the choice of sheet material, to obtain the best balance between rapid wearing of the pencil point with the need for constant resharpening, and producing the densest possible mark on the surface. Pencils are graded, I believe, from 6B at the softest to 9H at the hardest, though the uses of those at the extreme poles are beyond my own experience, and are confined to specialised classes of work. Obviously, it is difficult for different manufacturers to produce grades of identical hardness with one another, but the better ranges of pencils are generally highly consistent within their own range. It is a good idea, therefore, once you have determined which make of pencil (or lead) you prefer, to stick to that make, so that you will always know what to expect from a pencil of a particular grade (plate 45).

37

The range of grades you employ depends on the nature of the drawing surface, since tracing papers and films wear down a point far quicker than cartridge. You may want to set out finished drawings in a softer pencil than that used for finishing, so that errors can be more easily erased. Reversion to a softer lead for lettering may be a help, as it is difficult to 'drive' a hard pencil in the more complex patterns required for lettering, without scratching the paper-surface. Broadly, my own choice of pencil grades is as follows:

	Setting out grids etc	Main lines of drawing	Lettering
On tracing paper	H	2H	H
On cartridge	HB	H	F or HB

I think the golden rule with pencil drawing is to use the softest grade of pencil for a particular job that your own style of drawing and degree of neatness will allow. As to whether you use wood pencils or clutch pencils this is entirely a matter of personal preference. A clutch pencil feels hard and mechanical, but its weight and balance do not alter, and it is a good deal easier to sharpen than a wood pencil – but far less satisfying to chew!

(iii) Tone wash I was taught at an early age how to apply water colour washes, and have never subsequently understood why many draughtsmen regard them with a kind of awe. Putting on washes is by no means difficult, although it does demand a certain dexterity and a degree of confidence. The whole process is admirably explained by Fraser Reekie and others. The absolute essentials are, first, to make sure that the colours you are using are not of a kind that rapidly separates out (as this causes irremediable variations in tone), second, to mix enough colour for the whole wash (that is to say about twice as much as you think you need), third, to work in bands of colour from left to right, using the largest brush you can control and keeping a generous reservoir of colour constantly on the paper, along the bottom of the washed area. It helps to some extent to work on a damped surface, particularly if you aim to grade the wash at all – but this technique has only limited applications to measured work (plate 46).

(iv) Felt pen I use felt pen rather sparingly in measured drawings. It tends not to produce a uniformly dense black on tracings which are to be reproduced, and colours reproduce very unevenly. I do on occasion find it useful for thickening section lines and filling in substantial black areas in drawings, and even for executing lettering, in particular titles of drawings where very bold lettering is required.

(v) Tone films A wide range of prepared films with both tones and textures is obtainable. If you are in any doubt of your ability to apply washes, tone films make an admirable substitute, and indeed if flat tone is required on tracing paper water colour wash cannot of course be used. Some experiment is needed before they are used on translucent drawings for reproduction, since the printed grey tone of the copy does not always turn out as you would expect. Some colour films produce tones much darker than anticipated, others almost disappear altogether in the print.

a Setting out Setting out is best done on cartridge, thin tracing or detail paper. Use the biggest sheets your board will accommodate, so that you do not have to worry about containing the drawings within the sheet, and have plenty of marginal paper for establishing scales of repetitious measurements such as brick courses, and for setting out details to be fed back into the main drawings. This matter of details is important. It is often necessary to work out, say, a 1:20 plan and section through a doorway or window so that its main outlines can be transferred back on to the main plan, perhaps at a scale of 1:100, so both small-scale and large-scale drawings should be progressed together.

It is normally most convenient to start by setting out the floor plans. Whilst it is undeniable that to neglect the three-dimensional nature of architecture is to miss the whole point of it, at the same time it is the plan of the building, which tells us most immediately what we need to know about its form and function. Moreover, plans are simplest, both to measure and to draw, and properly drawn plans help to draw accurate sections and elevations. You may often find it most helpful in setting out plans first of all to set up a dimensional grid, of bay-windows and centre lines, and this will form a convenient framework not only for determining the size of drawings, but for drawing up the plans in all their detail. Construction lines showing the centres of windows and doors are particularly valuable in relating inside to outside dimensions. It is difficult to achieve total accuracy in site-measuring, and the establishment of these axes prevent many headaches in drawing up. I do not normally expect setting out plans to be a long and complicated task, except in those cases where buildings are not rectilinear, the shape of each individual cell has to be determined by plotting the diagonals taken on site, and the whole plan must be gradually built up, one cell at a time, with judicious cross-reference with the external dimensions of the whole (plate 52).

Once the plans are complete, a solid basis is available for the construction of sections and elevations. Provided the scales are common, the horizontal dimensions of these can be traced direct from the plans, taking care whenever drawings are removed from the board, that when they are repositioned they are properly aligned with the Tee-square – a matter I find absurdly easy to get slightly wrong, with disastrous results often only apparent at a much later stage of the work. I have suggested the use of orthographic projection for on-site drawing of details, but it cannot readily be extended to architectural drawings in general in view of the limitations of sheet sizes. Tracing horizontal dimensions from plans to sections and elevations, however, has the same effect (plate 53). The sections should perhaps precede the elevations, since the latter are in a sense generated by them. On sections, with wall positions etc traced from plans, the floor levels should then be added, producing the basic 'box' of the building, before window and door profiles, staircases and so forth are drawn in. Where the exterior of the building is of brick, I invariably at this stage put in on the margin of each section a vertical scale of brick-courses derived from the site survey, and annotate this to show window sill and lintel heights and the position of other elevational features such as eaves, cornices and band courses. Some draughtsmen, incidentally, seem to have trouble in setting out scales of this kind, for

43

brick courses and for other repetitive dimensions such as stair treads and risers. The essence of this (fig. 17), is to regard the scale in this context simply as a device for dividing a known dimension into a given number of equal parts. It is possible to obtain a very neat device (fig. 18) designed to draw parallel lines at any spacing selected by the draughtsman, and if you can get one of these you will find the drawing of brick and other coursed work much facilitated.

Provided that no awful errors have been made in the survey which cannot be detected by inspection, the section of the building emerges readily from the plotting of these heights over tracings of horizontal dimensions. The bones of the elevations can then be built up in similar fashion. In setting out elevations we come to more purely artistic problems like the reproduction of decorative features, carved work, tracery and the orders. Here again it is most important to process the details and the whole together. Within the amount of construction lines necessary to produce elaborate tracery, for example, I quite often resort to inking in those parts of the setting out which are firmly established, so as to be able to erase unwanted pencil lines and reduce confusion. It is sometimes a temptation at this stage to cut corners and embark on the finished drawing, with the setting out not entirely complete. If I succumb to this temptation I always regret it, as I invariably at a later stage uncover some fundamental error which requires the whole drawing to be redrawn. Not until setting out is complete should a serious start be made on the final drawings, apart perhaps from very large scale details, which can reasonably be set aside as a separate and self-contained part of the work (plate 54).

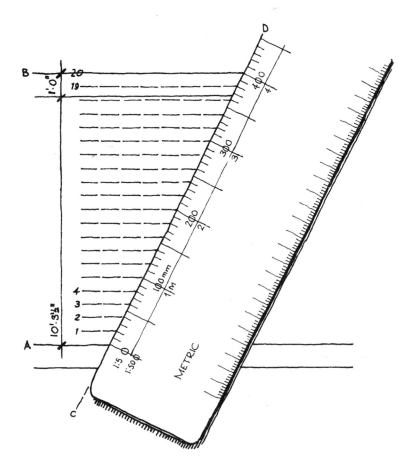

Fig 17 Setting out stair risers.
Drawn horizontal lines from A and B representing the floor levels. Using any convenient scale (not necessarily that of the drawing), place the scale obliquely so that the number of graduations on the scale is an exact multiple of the number of risers, in this example 20 risers, 40 graduations, and mark off tread positions as indicated by the broken lines.

Fig 18 Template for setting out stair risers, brick courses etc.
The type shown is the Linex 1007 Parallelograph. Rotating the circle alters the vertical spacing of the small holes in it.

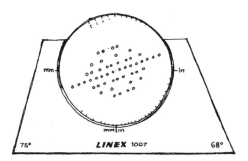

44

b Tracing and copying

If your final drawings are to be on tracing paper and film, you can now embark in a simple, 'down-hill' task which in my view, contains much of the enjoyment and little of the difficulty of the whole task. You are free to concentrate entirely on the neatness, clarity, consistency and artistic quality of the drawing. If, on the other hand, you are working on an opaque surface, you have the intermediate stage, of copying the setting-out drawings, to go through before the final drawing can be done. This process is much more trying. You must work as lightly as possible, particularly if your finished work is to be in pencil, which does not allow the easy erasure of construction lines, and if you are planning to use wash the drawing surface must be kept scrupulously clean. At the same time, using as little unwanted construction as possible, you must transfer the whole of the setting-out drawing to the final paper in full, and without loss of accuracy. The method of working is common to both types of final drawing. Consistency is to be aimed at, in such matters as thickness of line, and means of shading. Stylistically all the drawings should clearly correspond, and form part of a homogeneous set. This is less easy than it sounds, and it is particularly difficult to identify plans with elevations, presumably because the category of information they impart is different, the plan being a kind of section, and the elevation being strictly speaking a view. Similarly, a consistency of treatment in larger-scale details is important. Be prepared to shift to a slightly heavier range of pens – large-scale work looks spidery and loses its coherence if it is drawn too thinly. I attempt to introduce some common elements into drawings to convey consistency. For example, the textures of stone or tile floors, provided they do not clutter a plan, can be drawn in a manner consistent with the brickwork or stone of an elevation. For small repetitive elements such as decorative ridge

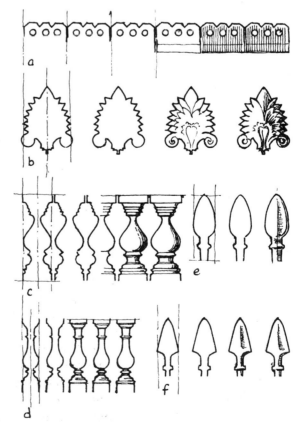

Fig 19 Home-made stencils for repetitive detail.
a *Decorative ridge tiles.*
b *Anthemion.*
c and d *Balusters.*
e and f *Railing spearheads.*
The stencils for these were cut from thin white plastic sheet using craft knife and leather punches.

tiles, pew ends or even elaborate tracery, it is worth cutting out a template in plastic sheet, in the manner of the stencils of bathroom fittings which are generally available (fig. 19).

It is sometimes advisable to execute finished drawings freehand. Where elevational treatment, for instance, is so decorative that a large measure of freehand drawing will in any case be unavoidable, it may be as well to elect to draw the whole without rule or compasses, as the combination of part-ruled, part-freehand drawing often fails to convey the character of the subject. In the case of full-size drawings or large-scale details, I nearly always employ a freehand technique, unless the original is very precise and mechanical in finish. Finally, I am convinced that drawing-up should be carried out as rapidly as possible, consistent with quality, since the more quickly a drawing is brought to completion the more fresh and spontaneous it will appear (plates 55 and 56).

4 Composition and layout

At the outset of my architectural studies I came by a large portfolio of printed plates on aspects of building construction prepared by the late W.R. Jaggard F.R.I.B.A. They looked a little archaic even to my inexperienced eye, and I did not press them upon my more forward-looking fellow-students. At the same time they had great appeal for me, as they seemed to present a lot of valuable information of a really down-to-earth kind, in a minute and interesting way. I have recently been looking at them again, for the first time for years, and find that they still have much of their earlier interest and attraction. The secret of this is the great care which has gone into the composition of each sheet. The style does not entirely come off – some sheets are overcrowded, and the lettering in my view generally too large, so that it threatens to dominate the drawings – but the best of the sheets make two points very clear. First, the representation of the three-dimensional nature of buildings, and the essence of the structure necessary to support the visible surface are perfectly captured. Second, the impeccable, economical composition necessary to good design, regardless of architectural style, should be reflected in a similar economy in the composition of architectural drawings. Indeed, the process of drawing in itself has much to teach us about the design of buildings (plate 57).

How is good composition to be achieved? There is no doubt that composition and layout are to a certain extent a matter of flair, of artistic talent. It is, for example, notoriously difficult to set out lettering solely by the observation of a set of rules. In the end the best graphic artists are those who supplement such rules by the application of an instinctive design sense. However, there are some pointers to guide us, whether the problem concerns the laying out of lettering or drawings.

Overall economy of space seems to me the first prerequisite. Whilst Mr Jaggard's structural details may appear too densely packed, it is far commoner for too much space to be left around a drawing than too little. Quite apart from giving the impression that the building is floating in an awesome void, over-large drawings waste paper, are difficult to store and to refer to. Plans or sections widely dispersed on a sheet are not easy to relate to one another, and the coherence of the subject is not readily appreciated. Therefore, compress individual drawings together slightly more than you think desirable, although not of course so close as to obscure the distinction between them. To achieve this degree of compression you need to know before the final sheets are drawn up the precise size of each component drawing. It is too late after you have begun to draw them up to decide to add a further section, or indicate the width of a street. Careful planning is therefore called for, and here the completion of accurate setting-out drawings prior to drawing-up is of the greatest assistance. An alternative, particularly when you wish to assemble a number of component drawings onto one or more sheets, is to prepare a 'mock-up' of each sheet to a much smaller scale, a sort of working drawing of the drawing itself, as it were. Each component is drawn in the broadest outline, cut out and shuffled like jigsaw pieces to obtain the most satisfactory composition (plate 58).

Whatever method you adopt, it is important that the component drawings on a sheet should follow a logical pattern. Plans should follow one another in ascending order, and elevations in sequence, as if the observer were walking around the perimeter of the building. Key features, such as staircases on plan, should align on an implicit grid on the drawing, so that the relationship of one storey to another can be understood. Different scales of drawings must be clearly marked. Finally, space must be left for titles and explanatory notes and every sheet in a series of drawings should be the same size.

5 Reduction and reproduction

Most measured drawings are probably carried out either as a preliminary to work on a building, or as a subsequent record of such work. They are prepared in the same manner as the design and working drawings for the job, and no particular thought is given to their reproduction by any means beyond those commonly available to the drawing office.

When, however, drawings are prepared specifically for reproduction, as illustrations in books or magazines, certain characteristics of the printing process have to be borne in mind if successful illustrations are to result. Indeed, it is as well to be aware of these characteristics when routine office drawings are being prepared, for you never know when the opportunity to publish may present itself. A very brief glance at the business of printing processes will help to define which aspects of a drawing determine its suitability for printing.

I have touched earlier on the way in which the establishment of sound printing technology made possible the accurate illustration of technical books, and referred to the difference between line-block (relief printing) and engraving (*intaglio*). Both these methods of printing line drawings survive, and remain in use in various forms. Nearly all modern forms of printing involve the use of the camera. Line blocks are zinc, copper or other metal plates coated with a light-sensitive film and exposed under a negative of the drawing. The resultant image in the film forms the basis of an etching process which removes the background, leaving the lines of the drawing in relief. It is clear from the manner in which the block is processed, that it is only applicable to black-and-white drawings entirely in line – there is no scope for any gradations in tone. For drawings in pencil, using shading of varying intensity, a 'half-tone' process is appropriate. Again the print is made from an etched block with the design in relief, but the image initially produced in negative form is broken into a series of dots by means of a screen in the camera. The spacing of the dots remains constant: in dark areas they are of large size so that they may merge, while in lighter areas they are very small, with a large area of surround. In highlight areas the dots are burnt out altogether, Between these extremes a complete range of tone is possible, and this is obviously appropriate to drawings in cases where techniques other than pure line work are used. Care needs to be taken where it is desired to reproduce drawings incorporating textural patterns of dots and so forth cut from commercially-obtained adhesive films. The clash between the screen size and the size of texture patterns tends to produce undesirable 'interference' patterns in the texture as printed, known in the printing trade as 'moiré effect'.

Both line-blocks and half-tones are relief methods of printing. Both have the disadvantage that since etching acid 'bites' indiscriminately, there is a tendency for the acid to attack the edges of areas left in relief, diminishing line or dot sizes. Moreover, long printing runs cause heavy wear on relief plates, impairing their quality. The modern version of intaglio printing, which avoids these pitfalls, is photogravure. The basis of the photogravure is a photograph printed onto a gelatin-coated transfer paper. This is applied to a copper cylinder and the paper stripped away. The remaining gelatin serves as the resistant agent during subsequent etching. Most gravure techniques employ a screen to form a network of fine lines cross-hatching the printed areas. This cross-hatching is converted on the cylinder into a series of minute pockets in the copper which hold the ink ready for transfer to the paper. Photogravure is capable of accommodating a wide range of both line and tone work, and of surviving long print runs – it is a process often used in the production of magazine illustrations.

Both relief blocks and *intaglio* rely on patterns sunk into the surface of a plate, usually by acid etching. Lithography is an alternative which exploits a different principle. The parent process, perfected about the end of the eighteenth century, involves the drawing of a design on a stone slab in a greasy crayon. The slab being then wetted, ink will adhere to the greasy design but not to the plain stone, and the design can thus be transferred. In photo-lithography, the design is again transferred to the plate, usually of zinc or aluminium, by a photographic process, leaving a 'greasy' image on the plate. Prints are taken from the plate with the non-image parts protected by wetting. Photo-litho is thus a process in which the image is neither embossed nor engraved, but is represented by a change in the constitution of a flat surface. This allows very subtle variations in the tone and texture of the original to be recaptured in the reproduction. All forms of pencil, pen, wash and allied techniques can be reproduced successfully.

It is not worth getting too bogged down in worrying about fitting the drawing to a particular printing process, for it is the responsibility of the printer to determine the best method of reproduction for the drawings with which he is presented, within the limits of practicability and cost. At the same time, acquaintance with the processes readily available, and in particular, the process appropriate to a particular medium, will save you from the embarrassment of asking for the impossible.

Common to all these printing processes is the business of reduction. Hardly any drawings are printed the same size as the original, chiefly I suppose because it is inconvenient for the draughtsman to have to worry too early on about the final size of the drawing. More important, it is difficult to draw the fine tolerances, dictated by small plate-sizes, which can be easily detected by the eye. Reduction of drawings clearly reduces the scale of errors. The concomitant of this is that the original work should not be so fine that clarity is lost in reduction.

Most drawings executed specifically for reproduction are reduced to some extent; a reduction of a quarter to a third of the linear size is common, and a fifty per cent reduction in size would not be unusually drastic. Reduction takes place in the initial photographing of the drawing, and at this limited rate of diminution is surprisingly tolerant of fine lines and cross-hatching. At the same time it is good practice to keep hatching fairly bold, and to avoid lettering on too cramped a scale. At one of the art-colleges at which I made a brief appearance a studio-master had a reducing-glass, which could be used to obtain an impression of a drawing of about A3 size reduced to postage-stamp proportions. This severe test was of considerable help in developing an easy, open style of shading and hatching in ink (plates 59, 60, 61).

6 Errors and their correction

It may seem trite to suggest that the best approach to errors is to avoid making them. But it is true that in the field of measured drawing the most successful practitioner is likely to be the one who can maintain an unblemished consistency through a whole series of drawings.

There is no one route to success in this matter. Some of us are by temperament meticulous and others are not. Those who like me rely on flair combined with cussedness for the execution of complex drawings require a more studied discipline than those gifted with flawless technique and unvarying precision. I can only indicate as pointers to the avoidance of error certain strategems that I use myself. Firstly, I regard it as of importance to make a false start! Just as a tennis-player needs to warm up before a match, and a pianist may be grateful for the opportunity to play some scales before embarking on a sonata, I find it very helpful to carry out some practice drawing before launching into the real thing. This preliminary drawing should be undertaken as if it *were* the real thing; if it turns out to be good enough to keep as part of the finished work so much the better, but I very often find I can swing more happily into a prolonged programme of drawings once I have made some mistakes and set them on one side.

If this strikes you as self-indulgent, there are more objective ways of avoiding draughting errors. It is well worth taking the greatest care in setting out drawings; when the final drawing is to be traced some latitude in the draughtsmanship (though not of course the precision) of the setting-out can be allowed. When you are setting out on the finished sheet, your work must be light, consistent and painstaking. Do not attempt to start any of the finished drawing, tempting though this may seem simply as a relaxation, until setting out is complete (plate 62). The completed framework of the drawing marks a most satisfying stage in the production of the finished work, and if carefully worked out to a high standard gives you an enormous amount of confidence to go ahead with the work of completion. In other words, the more comprehensive the setting out, the less demanding the finishing will be, and therefore the less prone to error.

It is moreover important to know when to stop drawing. Although as I have said continuity and spontaneity in drawing are best achieved by long, uninterrupted spells at the drawing-board, there comes a moment when sheer fatigue begins to induce error. Impatience with imperfections in your drawing equipment, a tendency to cut corners and ill-temper at interruptions are signs that to continue will result at best in a drop in standard of work, at worst in a spoilt drawing. For this reason it is most important to plan programmes of drawings well in advance where possible, and try to avoid the student's practice of too many late nights towards the end. The business of pacing yourself in drawing is of great importance. I seem to recollect reading that Pugin drew all the details for the rebuilding of the Palace of Westminster within six weeks – working on board a small boat – and he, alas, ended his life in an asylum.

Errors are of course inevitable. Sooner or later concentration will momentarily lapse, or the pen will flood. Sometimes they can be disguised. My favourite drafting error is in Dürer's engraving *Knight, Death and Devil* where the line of a horse's hoof drawn oversize has been elegantly converted into a blade of grass. Such artifice is not commonly open to the draughtsman concerned with objective recording. Clearly the correction of errors is much simpler in drawings which are to be reproduced. With the use of 'process-white' areas of the drawing can be obliterated and redrawn in their entirety. It is astonishing how far this process is carried by the producers of cartoons for the daily newspapers, for whom correction seems almost to become part of the art-form itself. The use of proper 'process white' as opposed to, for example, white poster-colour is urged as some photographic processes are intolerant of some white materials.

Ink work can also be reasonably easily eradicated from tracing paper. The most luxurious instrument is the electric eraser, a machine like a miniature power-drill with a cylindrical rubber in the clutch. Too heavy an application of this may cause the paper to be distorted, so large areas may be better erased by gentle scraping with a sharp blade, followed by 'boning' with a suitable implement (or a finger-nail) to repolish the paper surface and prevent the ink from spreading. This kind of correction cannot be used on cartridge and other papers. The only possible method of correcting serious error here that I have used with any success is a kind of surgical operation. The paper round the error is actually excised with a sharp knife, the incision made along any convenient adjacent ink-lines, and a fresh piece inserted, with an overlapping reinforcement at the back to secure it to the parent sheet. This extreme measure is not to be undertaken lightly, but those handy with the scalpel (or craft-knife) may find it less alarming than it sounds.

Finally, one cause of errors in draughting, in ink or at least of imperfections in line quality, is the slight build-up of grease on the surface of a sheet from repeated contact with the hand. This leads to imperfection in the quality of line, and hence to bad-temper and further error. It is a good idea to dust tracing paper lightly with french chalk before starting an ink-drawing on tracing paper, or even during the course of the work. Keeping the paper clean is a problem at all stages of the work. I generally have strips of folded paper attached to either edge of my board to lift the square slightly clear of the paper surface, and I think it worthwhile going to considerable lengths to mask out with paper overlays those parts of a drawing on which you are not actually working.

7 Lettering The days when many a good drawing was spoilt by poor lettering are long gone. Which is a great pity, because nowadays many a good drawing is spoilt by good lettering. By which I mean, of course, good transfer lettering badly applied. It would be a gross exaggeration to regard the past as a kind of lost golden age of lettering, but the fact is that when architectural draughtsmen relied on their own skills for lettering their drawings, many of them developed techniques which complemented their style of draughtsmanship. Characteristics such as boldness of line or meticulous cross-hatching became as much a part of the lettering as of the drawing, and imparted to the whole a pleasing integrity (plate 63).

Transfer lettering is in many ways admirable, and I use it often, but for labelling architectural drawings it does have some disadvantages. I suspect that in the first place it was not developed primarily for the architectural profession but for printers, graphic designers and advertisers, and as an aid to setting out lettering as much as to produce finished work. Transfer lettering has developed a long way since its introduction and the range of typefaces and sizes is astonishing. Many faces, however, seem to me strictly inappropriate to architectural drawing. I think this is chiefly because transfer letters are so polished, so meticulous and highly finished that they sit slightly uncomfortably with a drawing which is essentially a one-off, hand-wrought artifact. It is, indeed, the slight variations, the subtle inequalities and imperfections which, without impairing its value as a record of information, impart to a drawing an individual character which mechanically-reproduced lettering cannot, by its nature, match.

Moreover, most draughtsmen sensibly shy away from using the more delicate and spidery transfer-letter typefaces. These are much more difficult to apply to drawings than the more robust, coarser faces, and once applied are more susceptible to damage, especially on tracings repeatedly printed. Few draughtsmen, however, habitually draw in bold, coarse line with heavy black shading, and thus there is a tendency for the lettering to be bolder than the drawing which it announces. This is always a pity, because the drawing should never be dominated by its title.

If you must use transfer lettering, then it is important to choose a typeface which suits your style of drawing. Experiment with two or three kinds until you hit on a type which, at the sizes you need regularly, complements and does not overwhelm the general weight and mass of your habitual technique. Try to choose something which is stylistically neutral – avoid using old english lettering to embellish a Palladian elevation – and once you are happy with your choice, stick to it. This will not only save you the expense of a store of half-used sheets of different styles of letter, but will give all your drawings a kind of 'house-style' which will help to ensure that people recognise the authorship of drawings from your pen.

Transfer letters are of course only suitable for pen drawings. If you are finishing drawings in pencil you are forced to produce your own lettering. My own technique here is to produce a lettering layout on a separate sheet using either transfer lettering or an appropriate typeface from a catalogue, and then to trace the lettering onto the finished sheets. This results in the weight of the lettering matching the drawing, and moreover gives me the opportunity to place the lettering very precisely to obtain the best composition. I have been sufficiently pleased with this technique to start using it for nearly all my presentation drawing work, whether in pencil or ink (plate 64).

The beguiling 'extras' obtainable for use with transfer lettering, the people, dogs, cars, trees and so on, generally look out of place on measured drawings, and I think should be avoided.

Having said all this, those who can achieve a reasonable style should always be encouraged to develop their hand-lettering. Certainly it is not worth resorting to transfer lettering for the smaller wording you will need for notes on drawings, and stencil lettering even in the smaller sizes seems to accord ill with measured drawings. All architectural draughtsmen should be able to produce notes on drawings rapidly and neatly. The important thing is to practise rather than experiment. That is to say, search for a style and develop it. Successful hand-lettering depends on the smooth flow of the drawing instrument on the page. I switch to a slightly softer pencil for lettering, and with ink work avoid using too thin a stylus. Always letter between top and bottom guide lines – the grid on a backing sheet is an enormous help with this if you are working on tracing paper.

The success of all lettering, whether hand-drawn or transfer, depends on the spacing of the letters and the composition of the whole lettering block. Letter-spacing is very much a matter of practice, and individual judgment, but the essence of it seems to be to ensure that the areas of the white spaces between the letters in a word are equal. This is very different from spacing the letters regularly on a grid, as you will see that two adjacent vertical strokes – HI for example – need to be further apart than adjoining curves – OO. Some juxtapositions are difficult for the graphic artist to resolve – RA tends to produce a wide space, but curiously enough the worst nightmares – WW for example – do not in practice occur. With regard to composition, there is a historic tendency in architectural drawing to space individual letters and words too far apart, so that the wording becomes disjointed. Over-compression is a more serious fault, making inscriptions indecipherable, but is much rarer. Working out lettering on a separate sheet will enable you to avoid these extremes, and will make it possible to compose blocks of lettering symmetrically (plate 65).

Lettering is a matter of practice and patience. There is no doubt that poor lettering can distract attention from a good drawing, or that carefully planned and balanced lettering imparts an elegant and professional finish to a carefully drawn sheet.

8 Presentation　　The presentation of measured drawings, for whatever purpose, deserves consideration throughout the production process. It is as well to have a mental picture of the finished work at a very early stage. In a field where individual preference is of the greatest importance it is only possible to give an indication of the kind of questions of presentation which need to be resolved as the work proceeds.

Uniformity of presentation has already been stressed. The drawings and any accompanying notes, photographs and other documentation should have a clearly identifiable corporate style. All sheets should be the same size and preferably of the same material. The mounting of smaller sheets onto boards of equal size to the drawings is worth considering. It is a help if all the sheets are similarly aspected, that is to say, all 'landscape' or all 'portrait'. Lettering should be homogeneous, and sheets numbered in order and perhaps indexed if a large number is involved. The use of a specific size and form of presentation may with advantage be extended to more than a single set of drawings, to develop a recognisable individual style. This can be as overt or as restrained as you wish. Measured drawings are not primarily intended as eye-catching selling points, but a degree of uniformity and order not only gives a good overall impression of the drawings, but reinforces their credibility as an accurate and meticulous record of the building.

I have attempted to touch upon those aspects of preparing measured drawings which are susceptible to identification and analysis. I am bound to admit, however, that these aspects are to a large extent mechanical, and that they cannot be claimed to represent the essence of the art of drawing. Any drawing that is more than a purely mechanical reproduction of data is so personal a matter that once you have described the mechanical means by which it is achieved, you have come not to the end but to the beginning of it. The actual business of drawing cannot be described, any more than any other craft-form. Which is why, I suppose, when those who do not draw contemplate the work of those that do, the only question they are able to summon, in my experience, is 'How long did that take you?'

I have always found this question mildly irritating, but it does illustrate the difficulty of conversing on those aspects of drawing beyond the purely mechanical. I hope that draughtsmen will not be equally irritated by this book, and that they will find that it contains at least some information which will help them to avoid the avoidable pitfalls, surmount the purely mechanical problems, and proceed smoothly to the beginning of the drawing itself.

BIBLIOGRAPHY　　R. W. Brunskill, *Illustrated Handbook of Vernacular Architecture*, London, Faber and Faber, 1971.
Robert Gill, *The Thames and Hudson Manual of Rendering in Pen and Ink*, London, Thames and Hudson, 1973.
Harley J. McKee (for the Historic American Buildings Survey), *Recording Historic Buildings* US Department of the Interior, 1970.
Fraser Reekie, *Draughtsmanship: Architectural and Building Graphics*, 3rd edition, London, 1976.

LIST OF PLATES

Unattributed drawings are by the author.

1 Sebastiano Serlio. *The Pantheon*, Rome: plan. From *dell'Architettura*, 1546 ed. An illustration from one of the earliest comprehensive architectural treatises.

2 Andrea Palladio. *The Tempietto of S. Pietro in Montorio*, Rome: half elevation and section. From *I Quattro Libri dell' Architettura*, 1570. Palladio's great treatise had considerable influence in England, first on Inigo Jones and subsequently on Lord Burlington and his school.

3 Charles Normand. *The Temple of Minerva Poliade*, Athens: detail of angle column. From *Nouveau Parallele des Ordres*, 1819. A late instance of a parallel of the orders in which real and ideal examples from classical and renaissance sources are compared, to provide a reference book for architects and students.

4 Andrea Palladio. *The Temple of Hercules*, Tivoli: site survey. Annotated sketches made on site are generally regarded as ephemeral, and it is quite rare for early examples to survive.

5 Andrea Palladio. *The Temple of Hercules*, Tivoli: plan and section. A more fully worked out drawing prepared from the site notes.

6 Antoine Desgodetz. *The Temple of Vesta at Tivoli*: details of the order. From *Edifices Antiques de Rome*, 1682. The much vaunted accuracy of Desgodetz's work was impugned by later authorities including Soane.

7 John Soane. *The Temple of Vesta at Tivoli*: details of the order. Soane's interpretation of the same architecural elements as those illustrated in Plate 6.

8 William Chambers. *The Theatre at Herculaneum*: plan and section. Chambers was one of a number of British architects who studied and measured Roman antiquities during the eighteenth century.

9 Colen Campbell. *Lindsey House, Lincoln's Inn Fields*, London: elevation. From *Vitruvius Britannicus Vol I*, 1717. Campbell produced a series of folios of drawings from contemporary and historical sources, and included many of his own projects.

10 James Gibbs. *The Composite Capital*. From *Rules for Drawing the Several Parts of Architecture*, 1732. Not strictly a measured drawing, but illustrative of one of the many attempts to encapsulate the orders in an ideal form.

11 Giovanni Battista Piranesi. *The Baths of Caracalla*: plan. From *Antichita Romanae*, 1756. Piranesi produced many imaginative and analytical drawings of this kind.

12 Nicholas Revett. *The Tower of the Winds*, Athens: elevation. From *The Antiquities of Athens Vol I*, 1762. Stuart and Revett produced the first series of accurate drawings of Greek antiquities, which had a profound effect on the Greek revival.

13 Giuseppi Zucchi for Robert Adam. *The Temple of Aesculapius*: detail of doorway. From *The Ruins of the Palace of the Emperor Diocletian at Spalatro*, 1764. Adam employed professional artists and engravers to execute the finished drawings of his investigations at Split.

14 Thomas Rickman. *Church of St Michael*, Coventry: east elevation. Rickman was in the forefront of the architectural historians in the early nineteenth century who interested themselves in mediaeval buildings. He coined the terminology by which English mediaeval buildings are chronologically classified.

15 John Soane. *The Banquetting House, Whitehall*, London: front elevation. One of Soane's drawings awarded the Royal Academy's Silver Medal in 1772.

16 Charles Robert Cockerell. *The Temple of Apollo at Bassae*: detail of Ionic order. From *The Antiquities of Athens Vol V*, 1830 Cockerell carried on the scholarly tradition of Stuart and Revett. In addition to his excavations at Bassae, during his tour he established the form of *entasis* of Greek columns.

17 Francis Bacon. *Argyle House*, Stirling: the gateway. From *The Practical Exemplar of Architecture* ed. Mervyn Macartney. In this typical late nineteenth century book of architectural details, the illustrations deal in turn with different elements of the building.

18 F.M. Mann. *Shreve House*, Salem, Massachusetts: details of the front elevation. From *The Georgian Period : Colonial Details of Measured Drawings* ed. William Rotch Ware (*American Architect* 1904). Another turn-of-the-century exemplar, this time of American origin.

19 Ernest Goodman. *Trinity Hospital*, Mile End, London: section across the main quadrangle. From *The Trinity Alms-Houses*, C.R. Ashbee (Guild and School of Handicraft, London 1896). This monograph is the first ancestor of the Survey of London.

20 Frank Evans. *2 Palace Gate, Kensington*, London: plans, elevation etc. From *The Survey of London* Vol XXXVII. An example of measured drawing by one of the best known of recent 'Survey' draughtsmen.

21 John Sambrook. *73 South Audley Street*, London: ceiling plan. From *The Survey of London* Vol XXXIX. A further example of contemporary 'Survey' draughtsmanship.

22 J. Murray Kendal. *Eton College*, Windsor, plan. From *The Royal Commission on Historical Monuments Vol I* (South Buckinghamshire), 1912. A typical small scale key plan from an early RCHM volume.

23 (Unattributed). *Jesus College*, Cambridge: plan. From *The Royal Commission on Historical Monuments (City of Camridge, Vol I)*, 1959. The standard and format of draughtsmanship established at the inception of the RCHM volumes has been maintained.

24 W.G. Prosser. *The Barn at Darington Court*, Faversham. An RCHM record drawing of a threatened building.

25 W. Masiewicz. *Kelmscott Manor*, Oxfordshire: west elevation. 1968. A typical RCHM record drawing.

26 William A. Okazaki. *Single Brethrens' House*, Bethlehem, Pennsylvania: second floor plan. From *Recording Historic Buildings*, Harley J. McKee (US Department of the Interior, National Parks Service) 1970. Since the 1930s much of the recording carried out in the United States has been under the aegis of the Historic America Buildings Survey.

27 School of Architecture, Ohio State University. *Grant's Tomb*, Riverside Park, New York: south elevation. Ibid. Another example of the high standard of drawings executed for HABS, this time from a photogrammetric survey.

28 IAAS York. *Portchester Castle*, Hampshire: the keep, west elevation. Stereo pair of photogrammetric survey Photos.

29 IAAS York. *Portchester Castle*, Hampshire: the keep, west and south elevations. Accurate drawn elevations, one of which is prepared from photographs illustrated in Plate 28.

30 Nicholas Cooper. *Nunwell House*, Isle of Wight: ground floor plan. 1979. A further example of contemporary RCHM record drawing.

31 *Barretts Green Farm*, Hawkhurst, Kent: section. Because the building is decidedly out of level, the section is based on the establishment of an accurate horizontal datum expressed by a stretched line, from which all heights are measured.

32 *St Laurence's Church*, Hawkhurst, Kent: plan of the Warrior Chapel. A survey measured on site and plotted to scale, freehand over a reference grid.

33 *Court Lodge*, Frant, Sussex: first floor plan. A typical freehand-plotted site survey taken prior to preparing drawings for alterations to the house.

34 *All Saints' Church*, Hawkhurst, Kent: details of the nave and north aisle arcade. Site notes taken to provide information for a measured drawing showing a cross section through the church.

35 *Christ Church*, Kilndown, Kent: the chancel screen by R.C. Carpenter. The screen consists of a large number of bays of largely repetitive carving. A single bay is drawn to a large scale on site, and a reference grid established showing the overall dimensions (Fig 5). To make a complete drawing further notes of non-repetitive details e.g. lettering are required.

36 *All Saints' Church*, Hawkhurst, Kent: window details. A sheet of elevational details drawn and measured on the site. Orthographic projections are sketched of moulding profiles etc, and these are numbered and their locations identified by annotations on the main drawing.

37 *Saint Dunstan's Church*, Cranbrook, Kent: detail of ceiling boss. The vertical and horizontal coordinates of indentifiable points are measured and plotted and the remainder of the drawing is filled in freehand, by eye. Measured points on the right hand side of the drawing have been emphasised in this example.

38 *5 Crane Court*, London: heavily enriched mid seventeenth century ceiling on the first floor (GLC photo).

39 *5 Crane Court*; the same ceiling severely damaged by fire in 1972. A measuring grid of stretched lines has been superimposed to facilitate the production of drawings for the reinstatement of the ceiling.

40 *5 Crane Court*; full size freehand drawing of part of the ceiling prepared using the measuring grid.

41 *5 Crane Court*; one eighth full size drawing of the damaged ceiling, prepared from earlier photographs and the full size drawings taken on site.

42 *St Mary's Church*, Attard, Malta: west elevation. Ink drawing on cartridge paper, from a measured survey on the site, using stylus pens of various widths.

43 *The Victoria Hall*, Hawkhurst, Kent: north elevation. Ink drawing with brick courses etc in sepia and the remainder in black.

44 *Westwell*, Tenterden, Kent: Details of the front elevation. Graphos pen and ink drawing on hot-pressed paper.

45 *St Laurence's Church*, Ludlow, Shropshire: the choir stalls. Pencil drawing on cartridge paper.

46 Frederick Stevens. *Church of St George in the East*, London: west elevation. Pen and wash drawing on hot-pressed paper.

47 *All Saints' Church*, Hawkhurst, Kent: orthographic projection of elevational details. These details from the north side of the nave and chancel, measured on site, are set out in plan, section and elevation simultaneously, each serving as a check on the other.

48 *Clerkenwell Green*, London: montage of elevations. This drawing, prepared as part of a conservation area study to demonstrate the general grain of architectural style in the area, shows how glazing can be indicated in a slightly free manner with a broken black treatment.

49 *Cluniac Priory of St James*, Dudley, Worcs.: east elevation of the chapel. Part of a series of drawings showing the buildings reconstructed from a site survey of the extensive ruins and extant pictures of the Priory. Included to show how different materials can be indicated by stylised representations.

50 David Dancy, Jonathan Hill and Ian Tarpey. *Home Farm*, Shipley, Yorkshire: axonometric view of the dairy. A fine example of axonometric projection, executed in ink and monochrome.

51 Alan Fagan. *The Playhouse Theatre*, London: understage machinery; the upstage bridge: isometric view. This plate may be compared with plate 50, as an alternative method of projecting drawings in a 'three-dimensional' way. This GLC drawing shows the suitability of the isometric to explain the nature of complex machinery and its associated carpentry.

52 *Bedchester House*, Fontmell Magna, Dorset: ground floor plan. This and the following two plates show how a set of drawings is produced, each projection in turn helping to establish the next.

53 *Bedchester House*: section. The plan is reproduced in part on this drawing to indicate how the vertical lines of the section are derived directly from it.

54 *Bedchester House*: elevation. Again, the manner in which the principal lines of the elevation are determined by both plan and section are indicated on the drawing.

55 *All Saints' Church*, Hawkhurst, Kent: large scale details. These are drawn in ink, freehand with stylus pens of various widths, the freehand treatment being suitable for the complexity of pattern and the combination of straight lines and compound curves, and allowing for an adequate indication of texture difficult to achieve with ruled line or mechanical means.

56 *St Laurence's Church*, Ludlow, Shropshire: large scale detail of stall end. Again the subject is rendered freehand, but this time in pencil, affording more scope for subtlety in texture. This medium, however, reproduces less well (if at all) in line.

57 W. R. Jaggard. *Joinery Details.* From *Plates of Building Construction* by W. R. Jaggard (Architectural Press, 1929). A plate showing how the studied composition of annotated drawings may be taken almost to excess, but still produce a plate giving the feeling of a labyrinth of information which invites exploration.

58 *The Two Churches of Hawkhurst*: 'mock-up' composition of drawings for a projected wall-chart, showing how the composition and balance of the components of the sheet need to be determined with precision before the drawing proper is begun.

59 Large-scale drawing of stone-carving details reproduced the full size of the original ink drawing.

60 Part of the same drawing reproduced one half full size.

61 Part of the same drawing reproduced one quarter full size.

62 *All Saints Church*, Hawkhurst, Kent: plan. Part of completed setting out plan made prior to commencing the final drawing. The degree of detail to which it is desirable to go in the preliminary drawing is indicated by this example, in which everything which is to appear on the final drawing, apart from hatching, is shown.

63 E. Garratt. *Wrought Iron Door Fittings.* From *The Domestic Architecture of England During the Tudor Period*, by Thomas Garner and Arthur Stratton (Batsford, 1911). In this plate the draughtsman's lettering, in no way outstanding in itself, is nicely judged in weight, size and disposition to form an integrated whole with the series of drawings.

64 *Hand lettering developed from transfer lettering.* Each line is separately set out in transfer lettering, the lines are assembled onto a backing sheet and centred at the same time, and the finished work traced from the resulting block.

65 Richard Grasby. *Notes on hand lettering.* The subject is a wide one, but the plate encapsulates a number of important principles regarding annotation, letterspacing, the choice of typefaces etc.

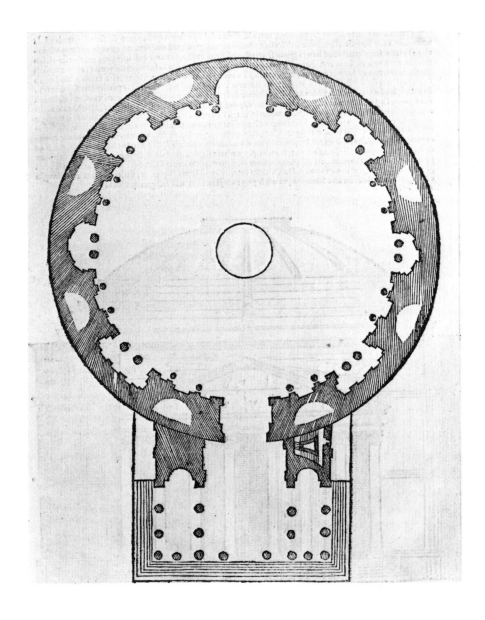

Plate 1

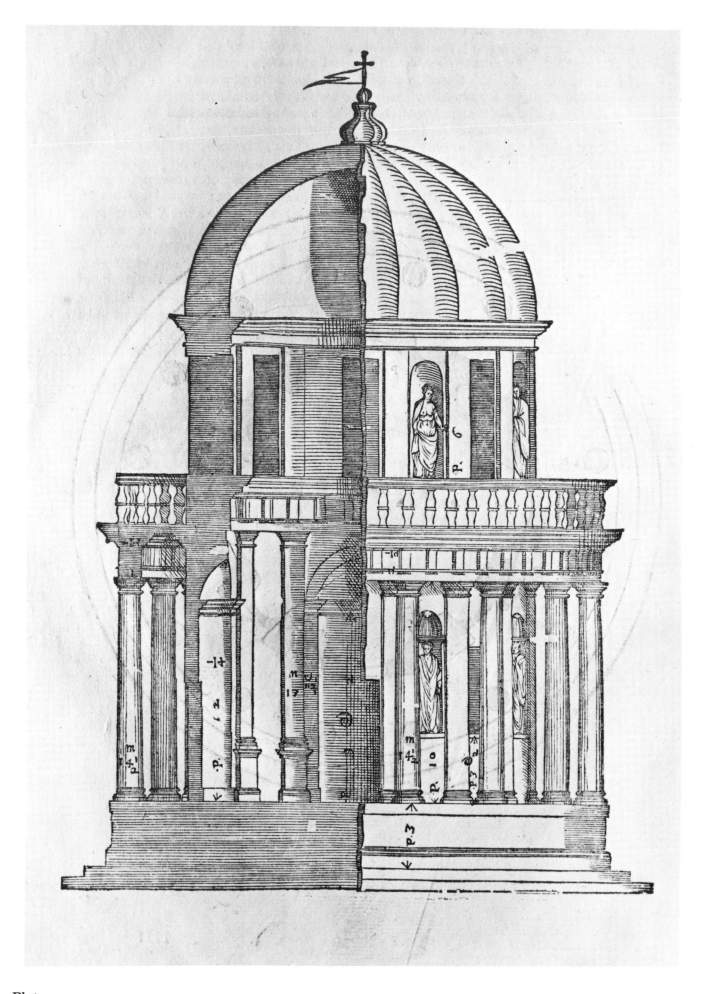

Plate 2   57

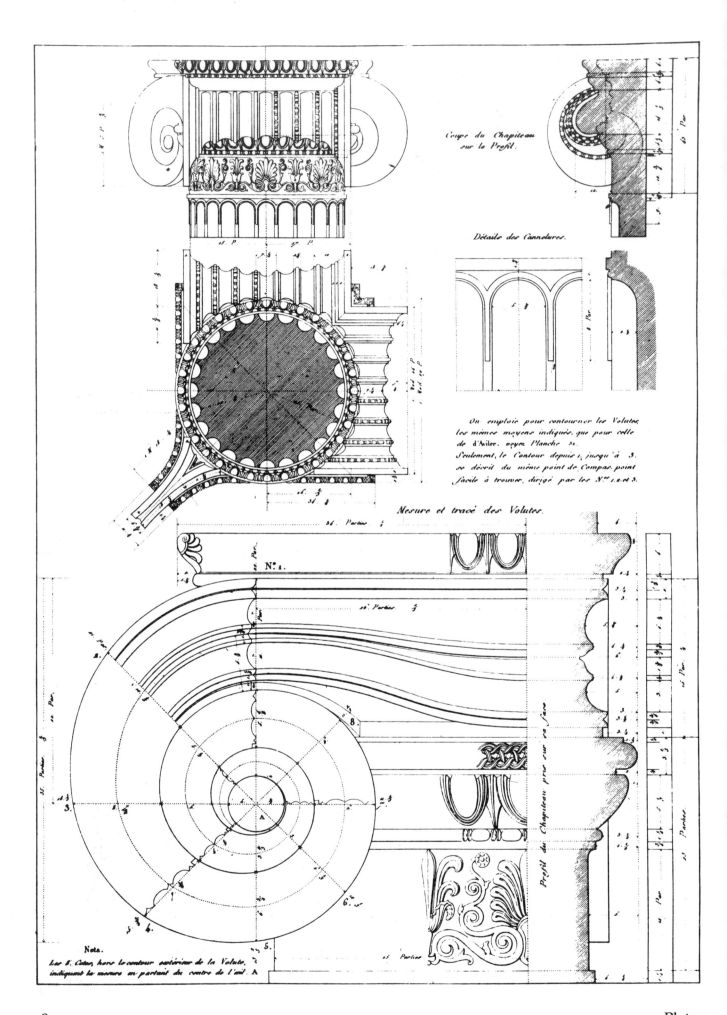

Coupe du Chapiteau
sur le Profil.

Détails des Cannelures.

On emploie pour contourner les Volutes,
les mêmes moyens indiqués, que pour celle
de d'Aviler. voyez Planche 31.
Seulement, le Contour depuis 1, jusqu'à 3,
se décrit du même point de Compas, point
facile à trouver, dirigé par les N.ᵒˢ 1.2 et 3.

Mesure et tracé des Volutes.

N.ᵒ 1.

Nota.
Les 5 Cotes, hors le contour extérieur de la Volute,
indiquent la mesure en partant du centre de l'œil. A

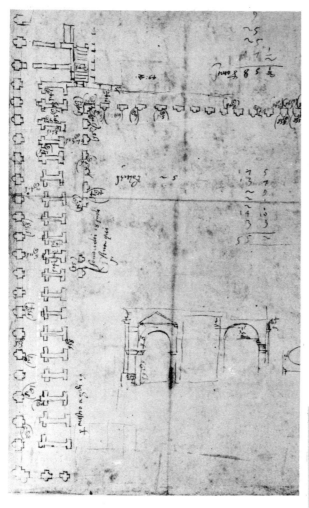

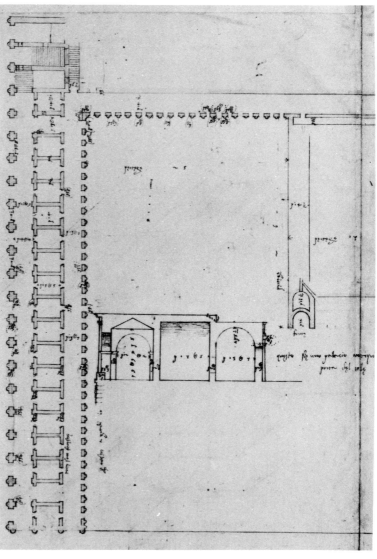

Profil par le milieu du Chapiteau des Colonnes

le diametre du bas de la Colonne est de 2 pieds 4 pouces
2 modules ou 60 parties

Base du Soubassement.

Corniche du Soubassement.

Descodex, del.

Prebos, fc.

B b

A·TEMPLE·AT·TIVOLI

Plate 7 61

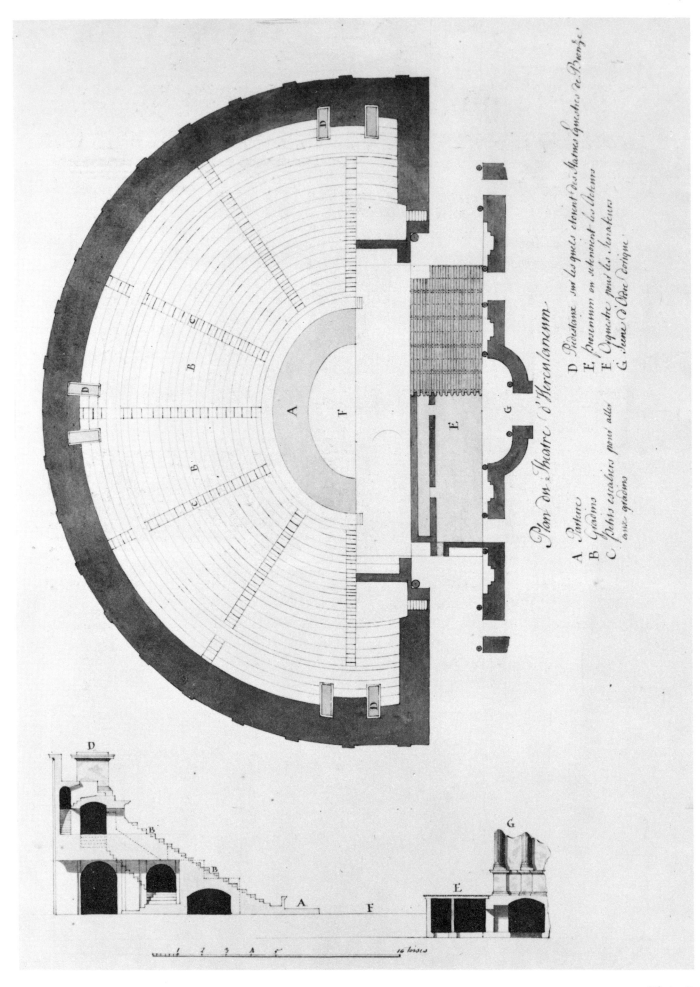

Plan du Theatre d'Herculanum.

A. Parterre
B. Gradins
C. Petits escaliers pour aller aux gradins

D. Piedestaux sur lesquels etoient des Statues equestres de Bronze.
E. Prostenium ou setenoient les Acteurs
F. Orquestre pour les Senateurs
G. Scene d'Ordre Dorique.

16 toises

Plate 8

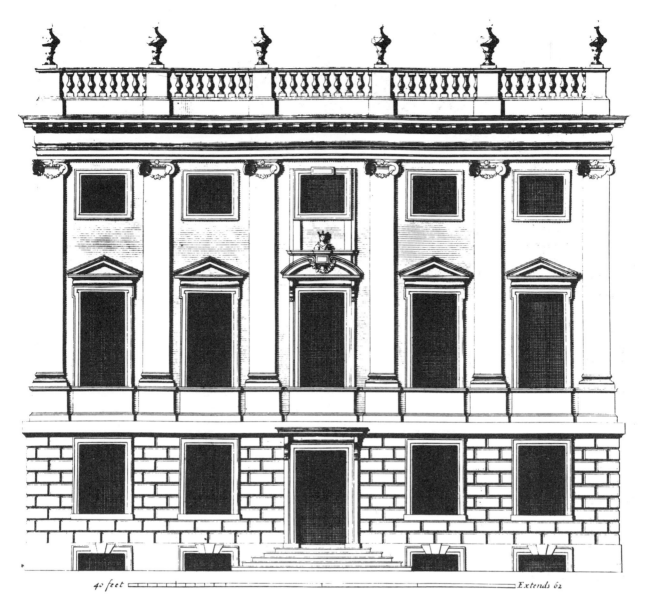

40 feet ———————————————————— Extends 62

The Elevation of Lindsey house in Lincolns inn fields, is most humbly Inscribed to the R.t Honorable the Marquiss of Lindsey Lord Great Chamberlain of England &c.

Elevation de L'Hostel de Lindsey dans la place de Lincolns inn fields a Londres.

Ca. Campbell Delin.

Plate 9   63

Plate 10

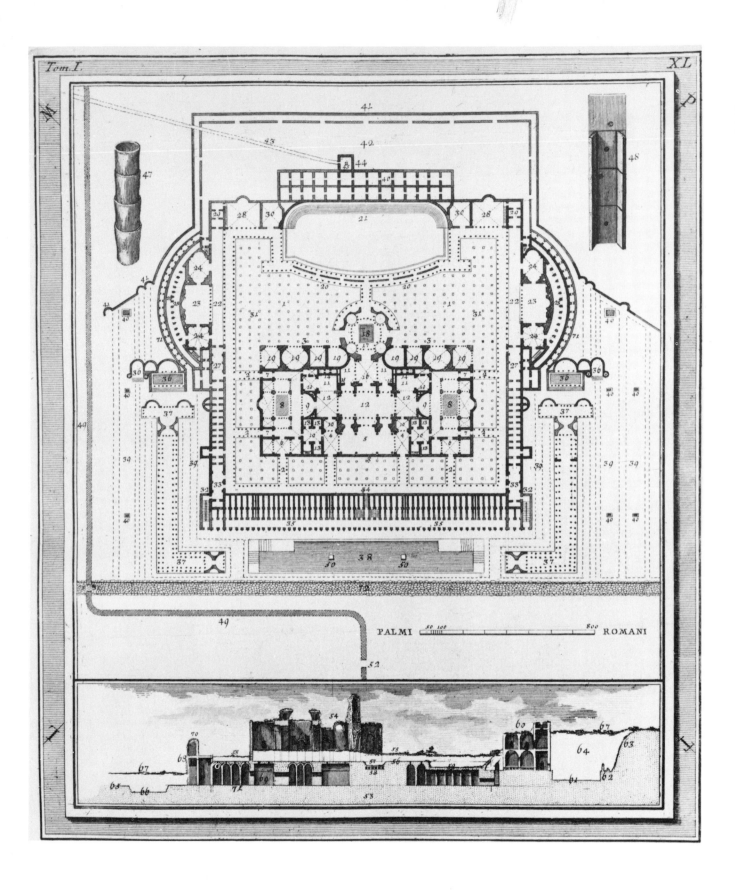

PALMI   ROMANI

Plate 11

65

Plate 12

Part of the Door of the Temple to a Larger Scale

A

Part of the Soffit of the Cornice

B

Scale of Feet

Zucchi sculp.t

Plate 13

67

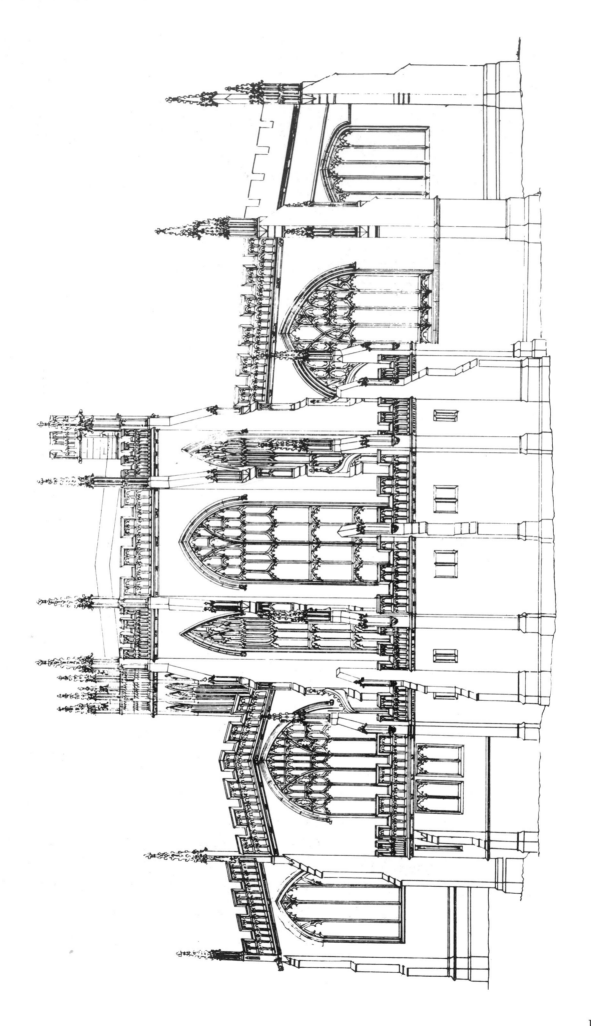

Plate 14

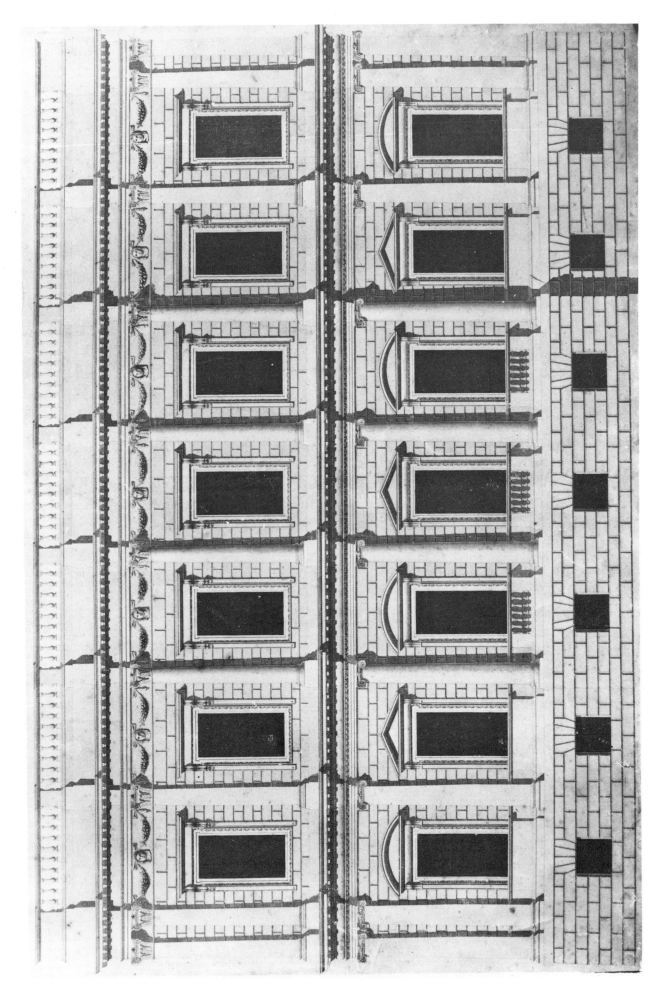

Plate 15

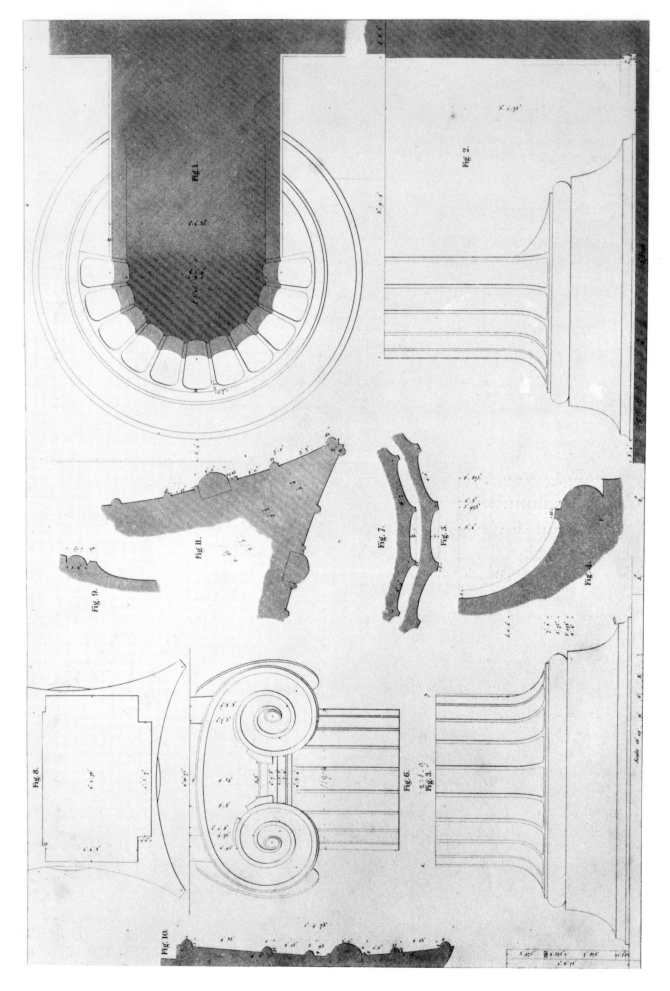

Plate 16

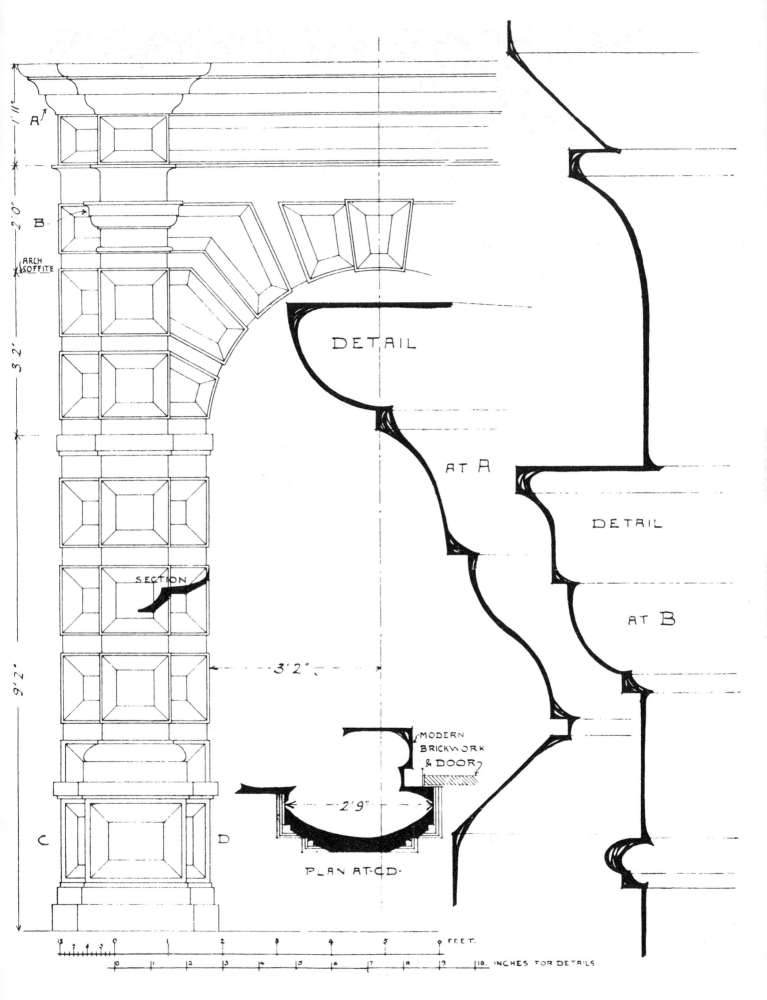

1'11"

A

2'0"

B

ARCH
SOFFITE

3'2'

DETAIL

AT A

DETAIL

9'2'

SECTION

AT B

— 3'2" —

MODERN
BRICKWORK
& DOOR

— 2'9" —

C   D

PLAN AT·CD·

5 4 3 2 1 0   2   3   4   5   0 FEET.

0   1   2   3   4   5   6   7   8   9   10. INCHES FOR DETAILS

Plate 17   71

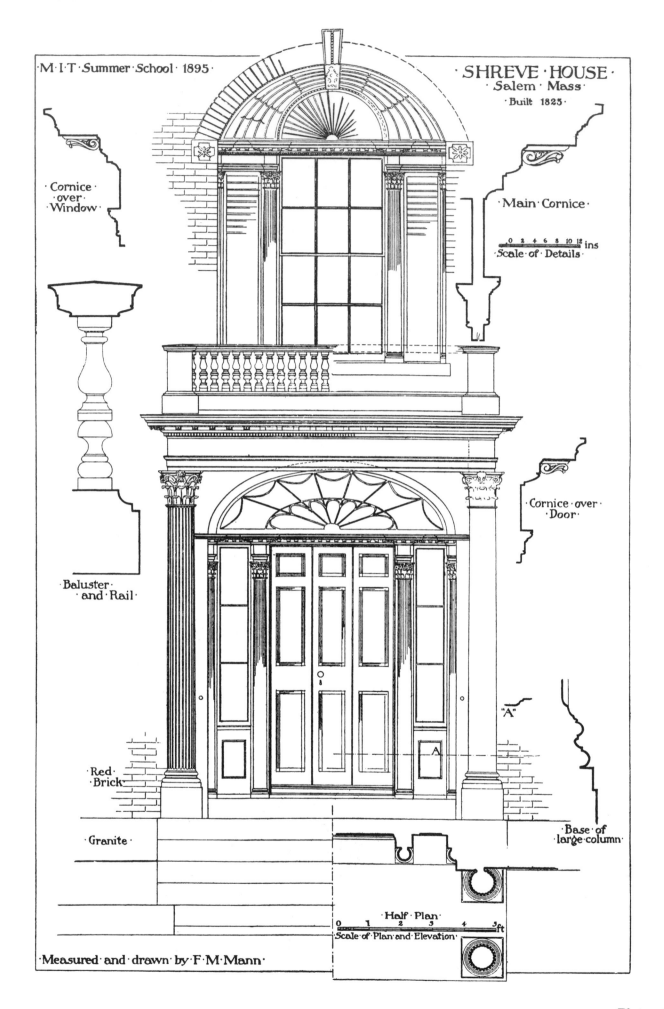

·M·I·T·Summer·School·1895·

·Cornice·
·over·
·Window·

·SHREVE·HOUSE·
·Salem·Mass·
·Built·1825·

·Main·Cornice·

0 2 4 6 8 10 12 ins
·Scale·of·Details·

·Baluster·
·and·Rail·

·Cornice·over·
·Door·

·Red·
·Brick·

"A"

A

·Granite·

·Base·of·
·large·column·

·Half·Plan·
0   1   2   3   4   3 ft
·Scale·of·Plan·and·Elevation·

·Measured·and·drawn·by·F·M·Mann·

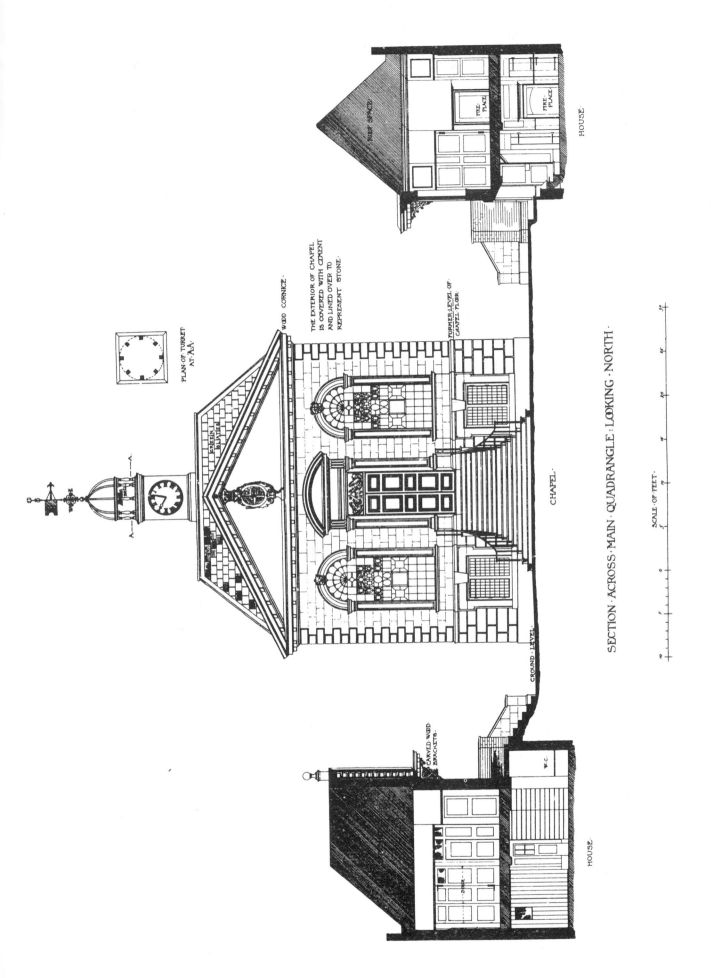

PLAN OF TURRET AT A·A·

WOOD CORNICE·

THE EXTERIOR OF CHAPEL IS COVERED WITH CEMENT AND LINED OVER TO REPRESENT STONE·

FORMER·LEVEL·OF· CHAPEL·FLOOR·

ROOF SPACE·

FIRE· PLACE·

FIRE· PLACE·

HOUSE·

HOUSE·

CHAPEL·

GROUND·LEVEL·

CARVED WOOD· BRACKETS·

W.C.

SECTION · ACROSS · MAIN · QUADRANGLE : LOOKING · NORTH ·

SCALE · OF · FEET ·

Plate 19   73

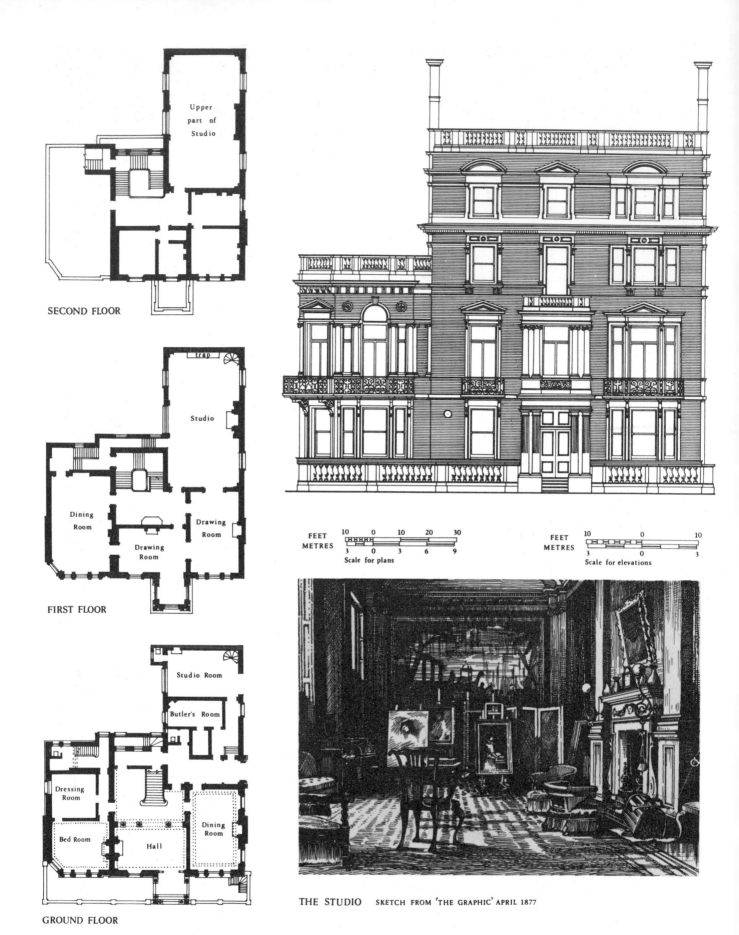

SECOND FLOOR

FIRST FLOOR

Studio

Dining
Room

Drawing
Room

Drawing
Room

Upper
part of
Studio

trap

Studio Room

Butler's Room

Dressing
Room

Bed Room

Hall

Dining
Room

GROUND FLOOR

FEET
METRES
10   0   10   20   30
3   0   3   6   9
Scale for plans

FEET
METRES
10   0   10
3   0   3
Scale for elevations

THE STUDIO   SKETCH FROM 'THE GRAPHIC' APRIL 1877

Plate 21

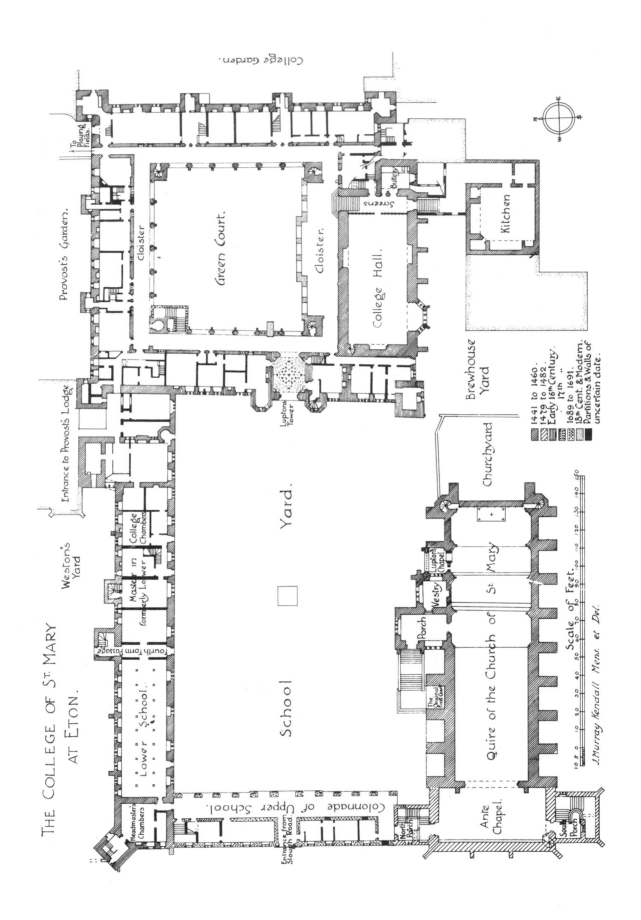

THE COLLEGE OF ST. MARY
AT ETON.

College Garden.

To Playing Fields.

Provost's Garden.

Cloister

Green Court.

Cloister.

Entrance to Provost's Lodge

Screens

Butlery

College Hall.

Kitchen

Brewhouse Yard

Lupton's Tower

1441 to 1460.
1479 to 1482.
Early 16th Century.
17th "
1689 to 1691.
18th Cent. & Modern.
Partitions & Walls of
uncertain date.

Weston's Yard

College Chambers

Master in formerly Lower

Fourth Form Passage

Yard.

School

Lower School.

Headmaster's Chambers

Colonnade of Upper School.

Entrance from Slough Road.

North Porch

Churchyard

Lupton's Chapel

Vestry

Porch

The Chapel yard Gate

Quire of the Church of St. Mary

Ante Chapel.

South Porch

Scale of Feet.

10 5 0   10   20   30   40   50   60   70   80   90 100 110 120 130 140 150

J. Murray Kendall Mens. et Del.

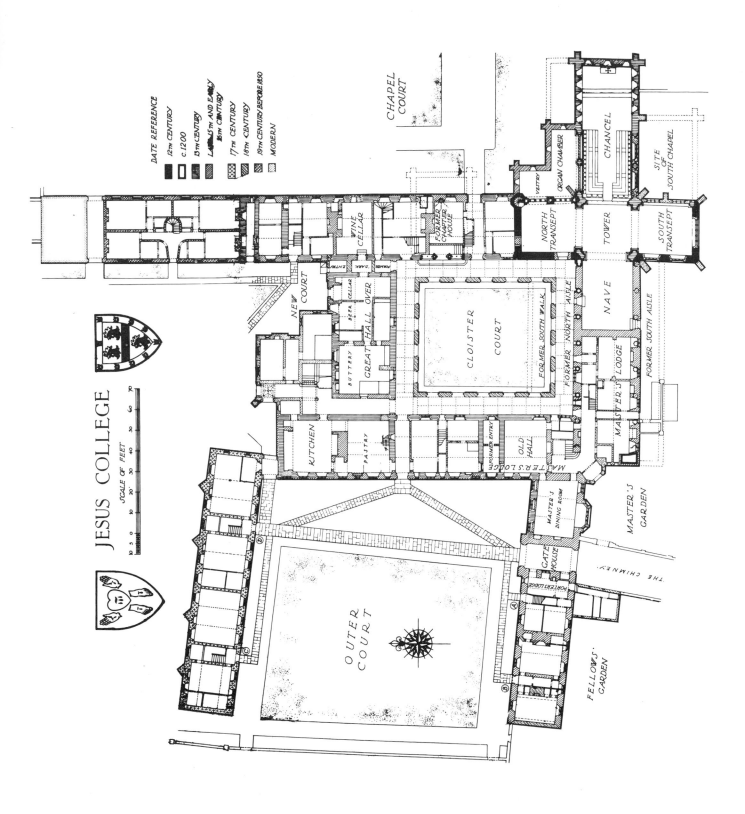

JESUS COLLEGE

DATE REFERENCE
12th CENTURY
c.1200
13th CENTURY
LATE 14th AND EARLY 15th CENTURY
17th CENTURY
18th CENTURY
19th CENTURY BEFORE 1850
MODERN

SCALE OF FEET

CHAPEL COURT

SITE OF SOUTH CHAPEL

CHANCEL

ORGAN CHAMBER

VESTRY

FORMER CHAPTER HOUSE

NORTH TRANSEPT

TOWER

SOUTH TRANSEPT

NAVE

FORMER NORTH AISLE

FORMER SOUTH AISLE

WINE CELLAR

CLOISTER COURT

FORMER SOUTH WALK

NEW COURT

BEER CELLAR

GREAT HALL OVER

BUTTERY

MASTER'S LODGE

KITCHEN

PANTRY

OLD HALL

FORMER ENTRY

MASTER'S LODGE

MASTER'S GARDEN

MASTER'S DINING ROOM

OUTER COURT

GATE HOUSE

THE CHIMNEY

PORTER'S LODGE

FELLOWS' GARDEN

Plate 23

77

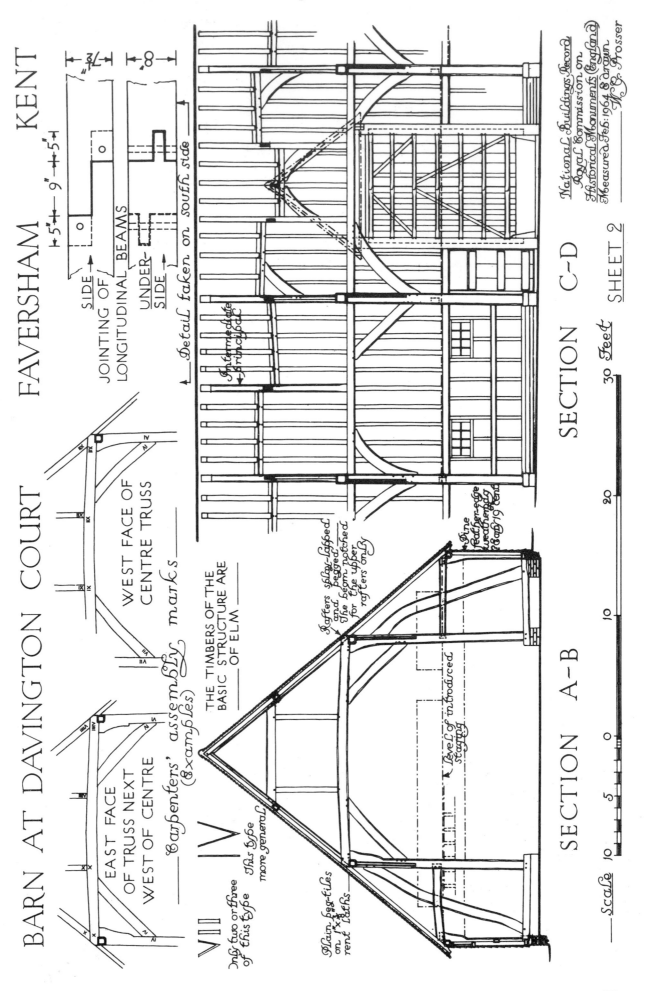

BARN AT DAVINGTON COURT   FAVERSHAM   KENT

JOINTING OF
LONGITUDINAL BEAMS

←5"→←9"→←5"→

SIDE →
←8"→
UNDER-
SIDE

Detail taken on south side

EAST FACE
OF TRUSS NEXT
WEST OF CENTRE

WEST FACE
OF CENTRE TRUSS

Carpenters' assembly marks
(examples)

THE TIMBERS OF THE
BASIC STRUCTURE ARE
OF ELM

VIII
Only two or three
of this type

IV
This type
more general

Intermediate
principal

Rafters splay-lapped
and pegged
The beam notched
for the upper
rafters only

Plain peg-tiles
on 1"×2"
rent laths

Pine
feather-edge
weatherboarding
18th&19thCent?

Level of introduced
staging

SECTION A—B

SECTION C—D

Scale   10   5   0   10   20   30   Feet

National Buildings Record
Royal Commission on
Historical Monuments (England)
Measured Feb: 1964 & drawn
W. G. Prosser

SHEET 2

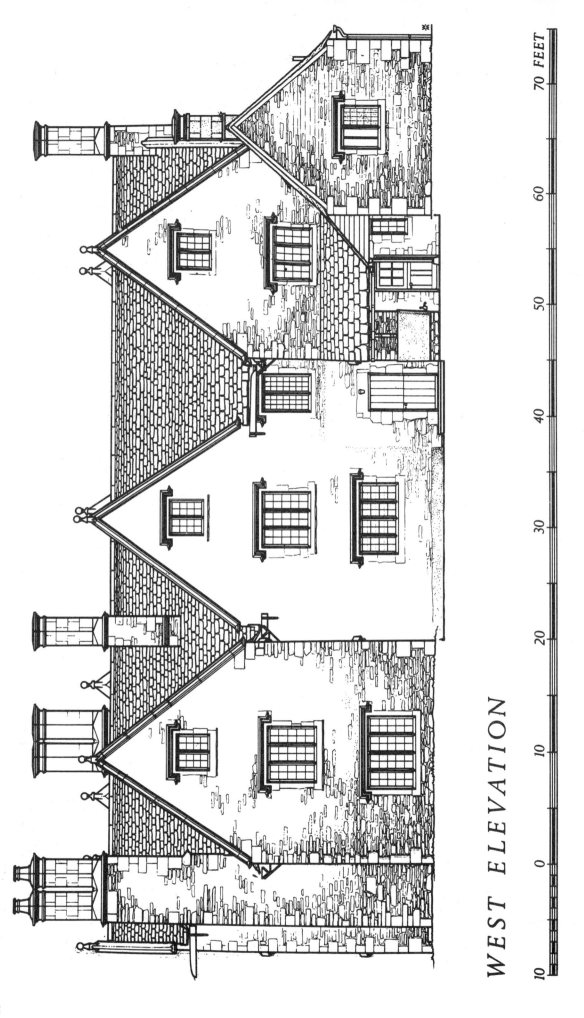

WEST ELEVATION

0 10 20 30 40 50 60 70 FEET

Plate 25

79

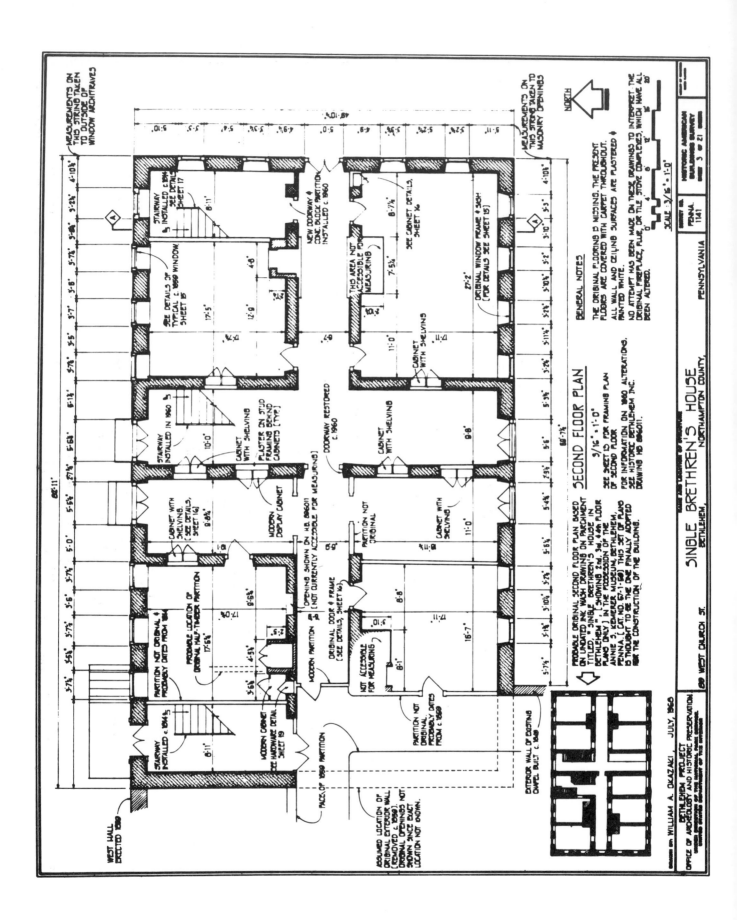

SECOND FLOOR PLAN

3/16" = 1'-0"

SEE SHEET 13 FOR FRAMING PLAN OF SECOND FLOOR

FOR INFORMATION ON 1960 ALTERATIONS. SEE HISTORIC BETHLEHEM INC. DRAWING NO. BR6011.

GENERAL NOTES

THE ORIGINAL FLOORING IS MISSING. THE PRESENT FLOORS ARE COVERED WITH CARPET THROUGHOUT.

ALL WALL AND CEILING SURFACES ARE PLASTERED & PAINTED WHITE.

NO ATTEMPT HAS BEEN MADE ON THESE DRAWINGS TO INTERPRET THE ORIGINAL FIREPLACE, FLUE, OR TILE STOVE COUPLEXS, WHICH HAVE ALL BEEN ALTERED.

SINGLE BRETHREN'S HOUSE
BETHLEHEM, NORTHAMPTON COUNTY, PENNSYLVANIA

80

Plate 26

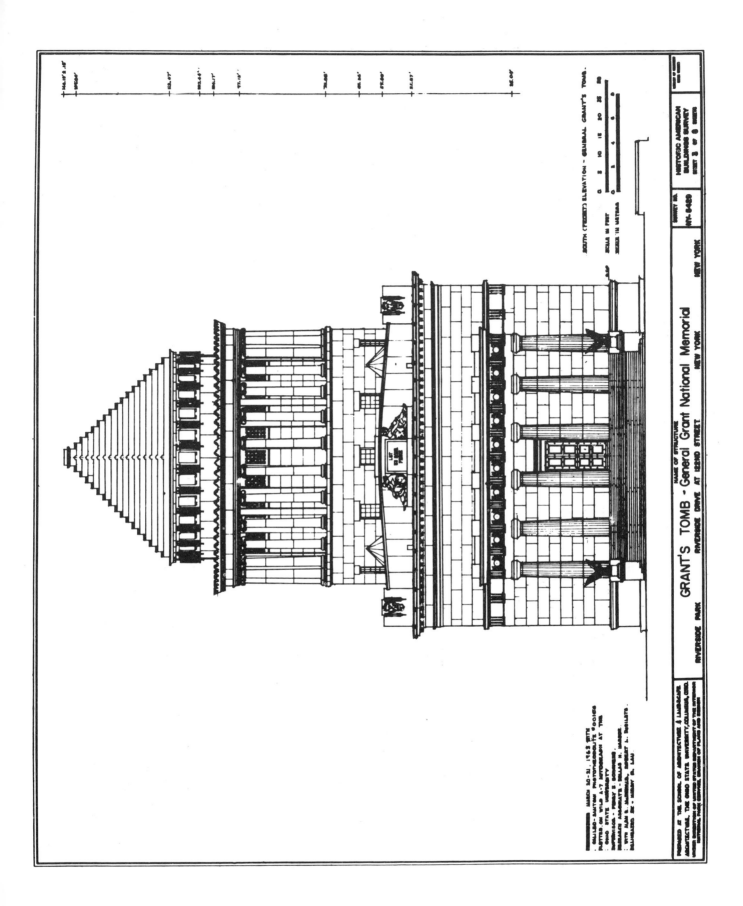

Plate 27

Plate 28

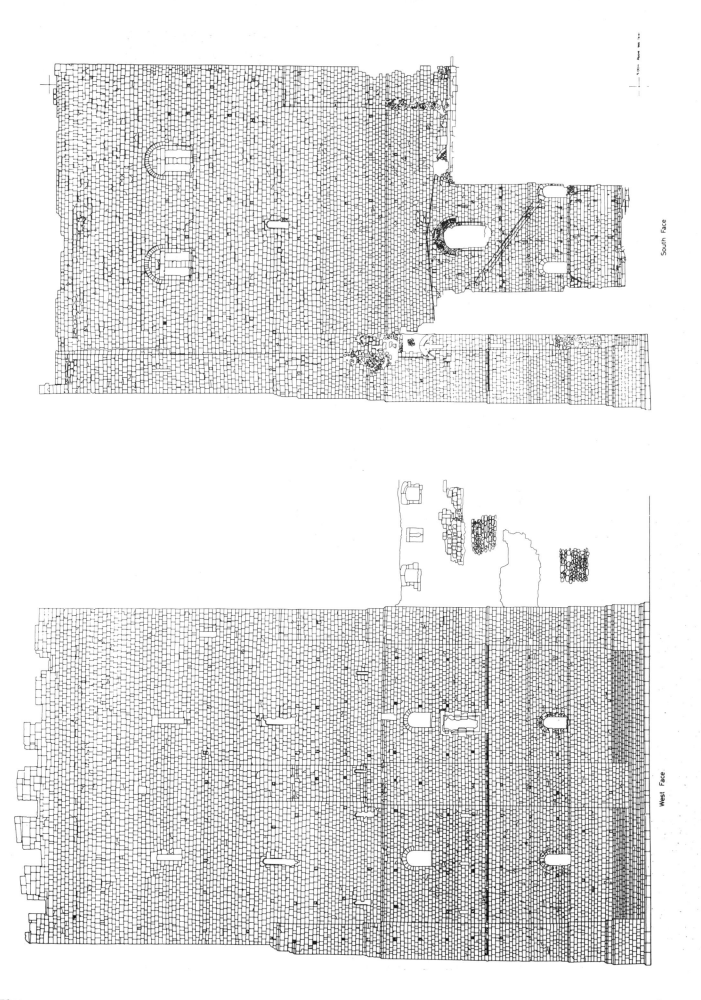

South Face

West Face.

Plate 29

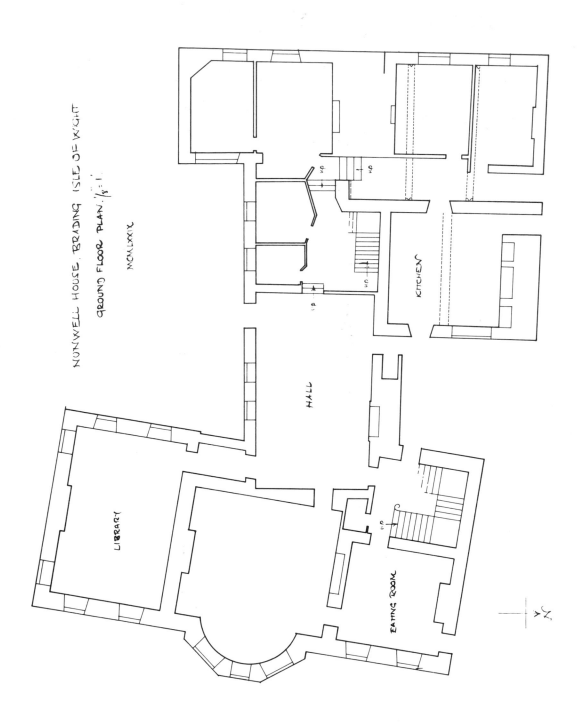

NUNWELL HOUSE, BRADING, ISLE OF WIGHT

GROUND FLOOR PLAN. ⅛:1'

MCMLXXIX

LIBRARY

HALL

EATING ROOM

KITCHEN

⅛":1'-0'

84

Plate 30

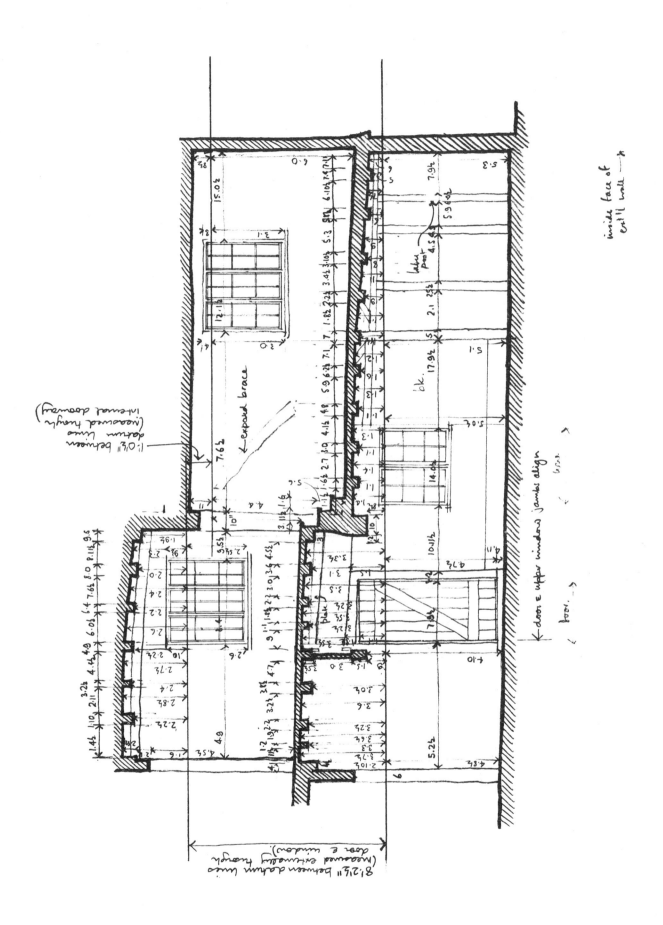

Plate 31

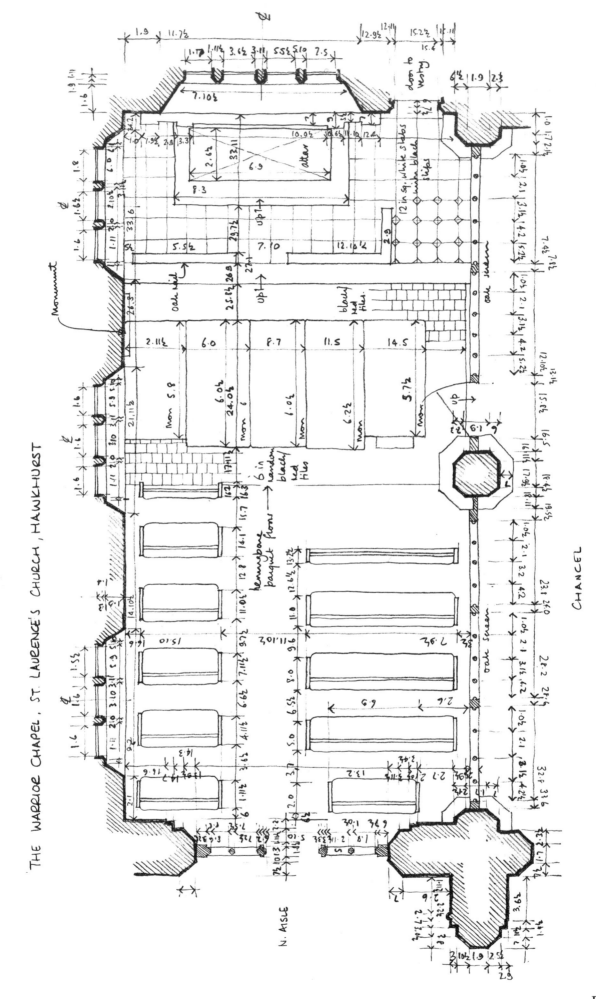

THE WARRIOR CHAPEL, ST. LAWRENCE'S CHURCH, HAWKHURST

CHANCEL

N. AISLE

Plate 32

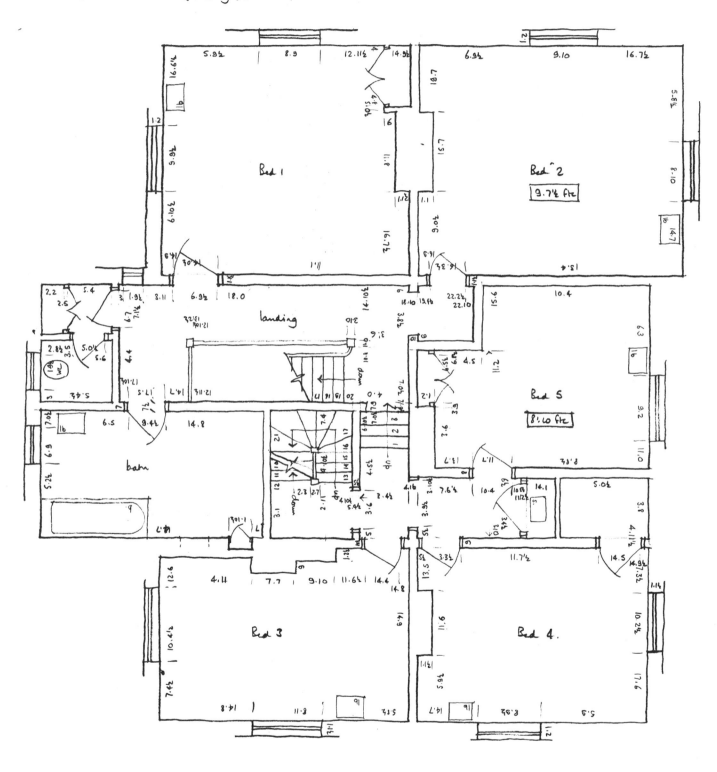

2'6" change of level between landings
11'5" floor to floor (front stairs)
9'0½" floor to floor (back stairs)
1'1" floor thickness (landing).

Bed 1

Bed 2

9.7½ fce

landing

Bed 5

8.6 fce

bath

Bed 3

Bed 4

Plate 33

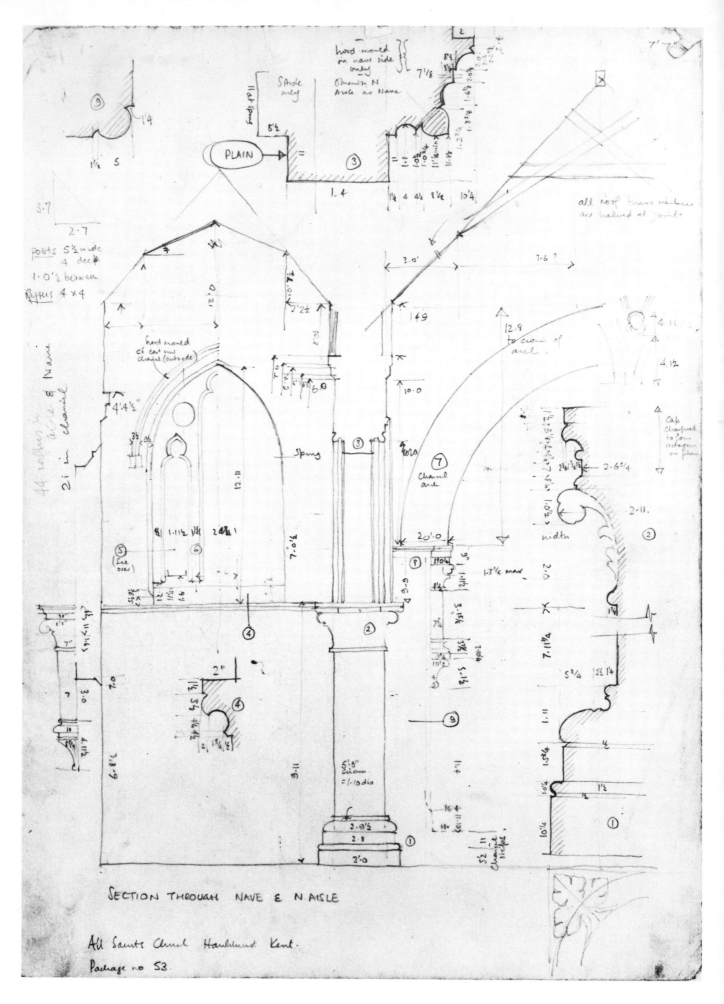

SECTION THROUGH NAVE & N. AISLE

All Saints Church Hawkhurst Kent.
Package no 53.

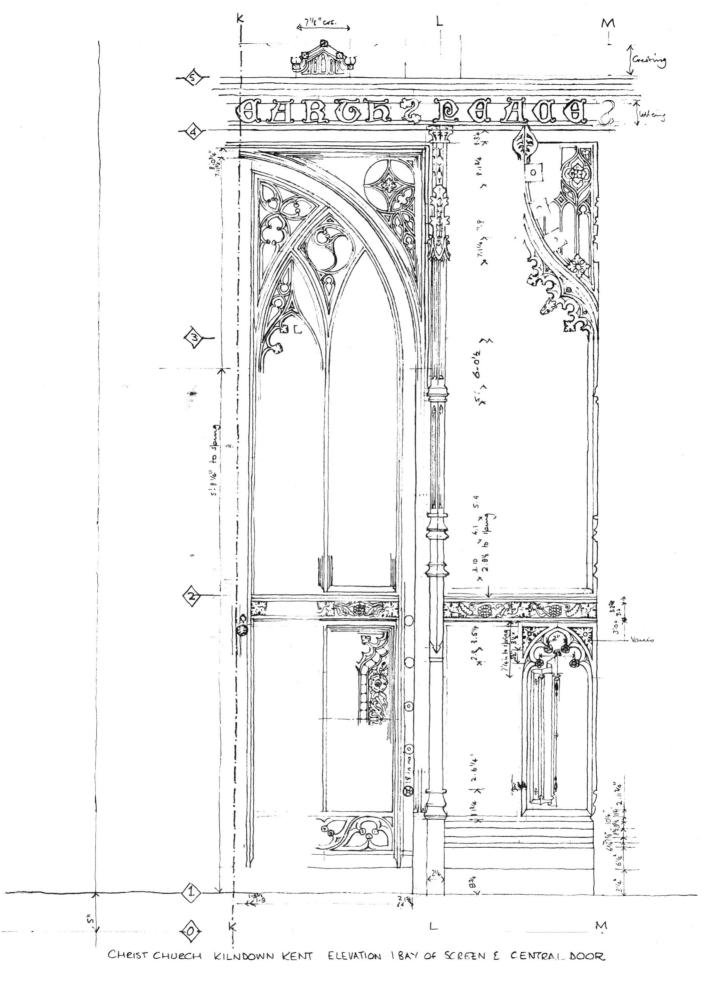

CHRIST CHURCH KILNDOWN KENT ELEVATION 1 BAY OF SCREEN & CENTRAL DOOR

Plate 35

89

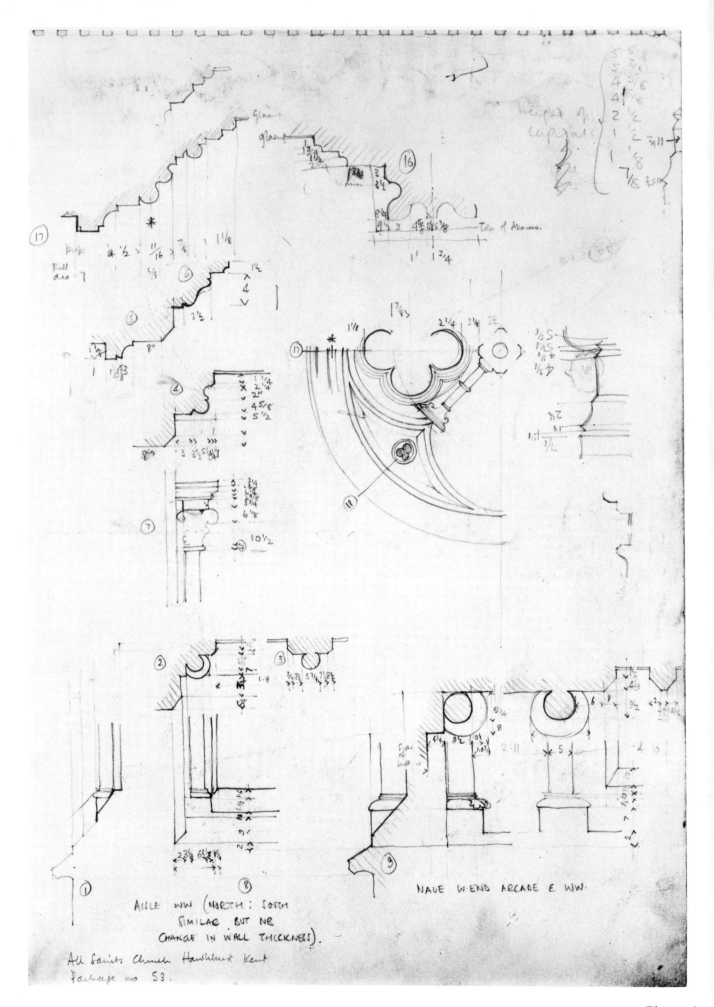

AISLE WW (NORTH : SOUTH
SIMILAR BUT NR
CHANGE IN WALL THICKNESS).

NAVE W END ARCADE E WW.

All Saints Church Hawkhurst Kent
Package no 53.

Plate 36

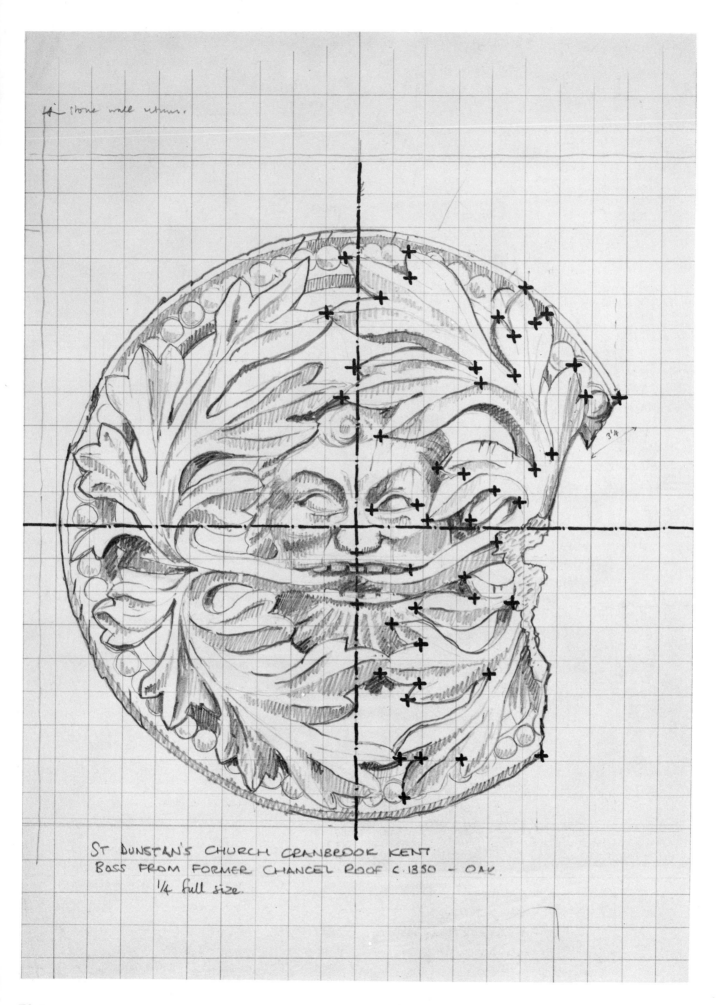

St Dunstan's Church Cranbrook Kent
Boss from former chancel roof c. 1350 - oak.
1/4 full size.

Plate 37

91

Plate 38

Plate 39

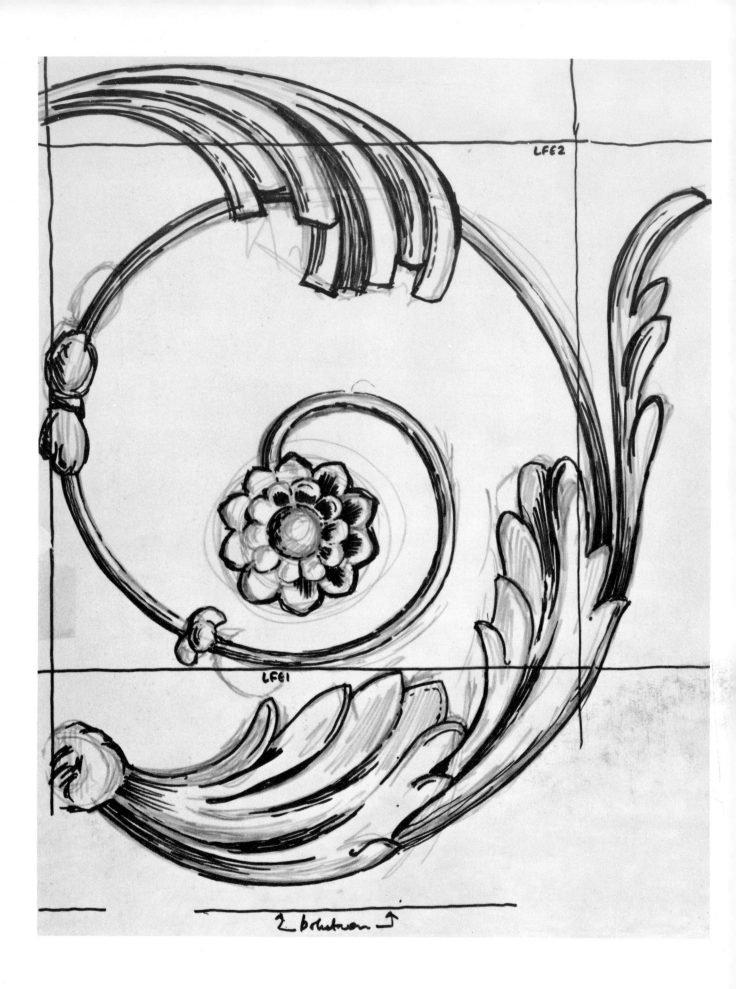

Plate 40

limit of cornice

Plate 41

95

scale

1 0 1 2 3 4 5 6 7 8 9 10 11 12

Plate 42

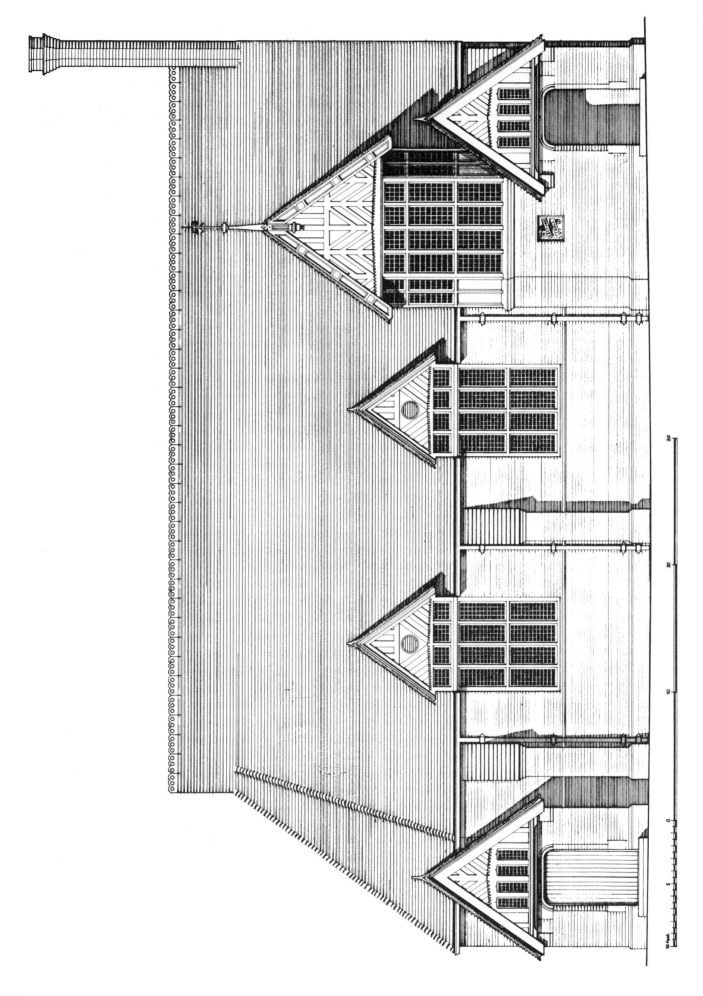

Plate 43

97

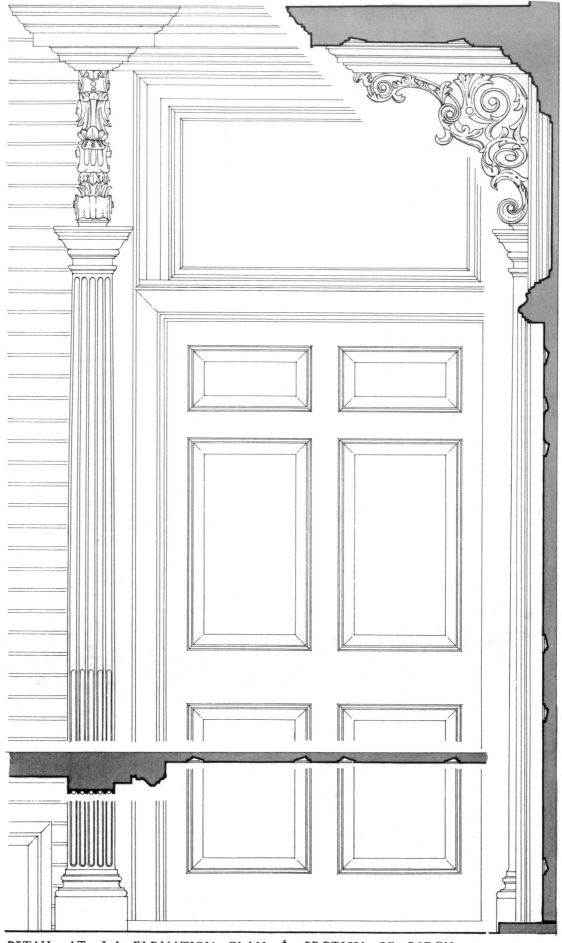

DETAIL AT J : ELEVATION, PLAN & SECTION OF PORCH

Plate 44

SHEET 2   DETAILS OF STALLS, NORTH SIDE OF CHOIR

ST. LAURENCE'S CHURCH, LUDLOW

THE CHOIR STALLS

Scale

Plate 45   99

Plate 46

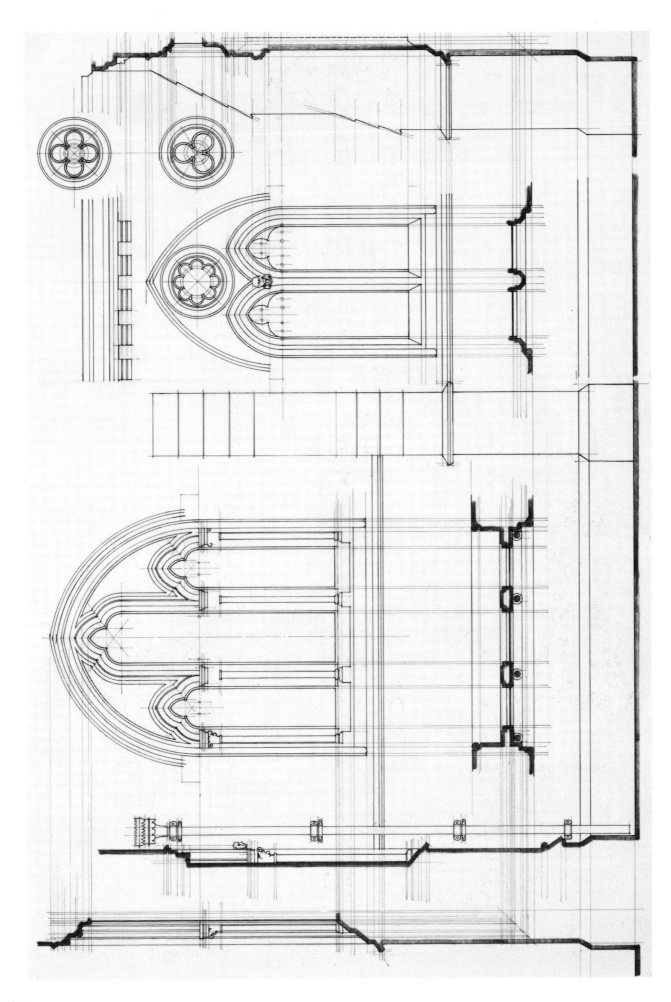

Plate 47

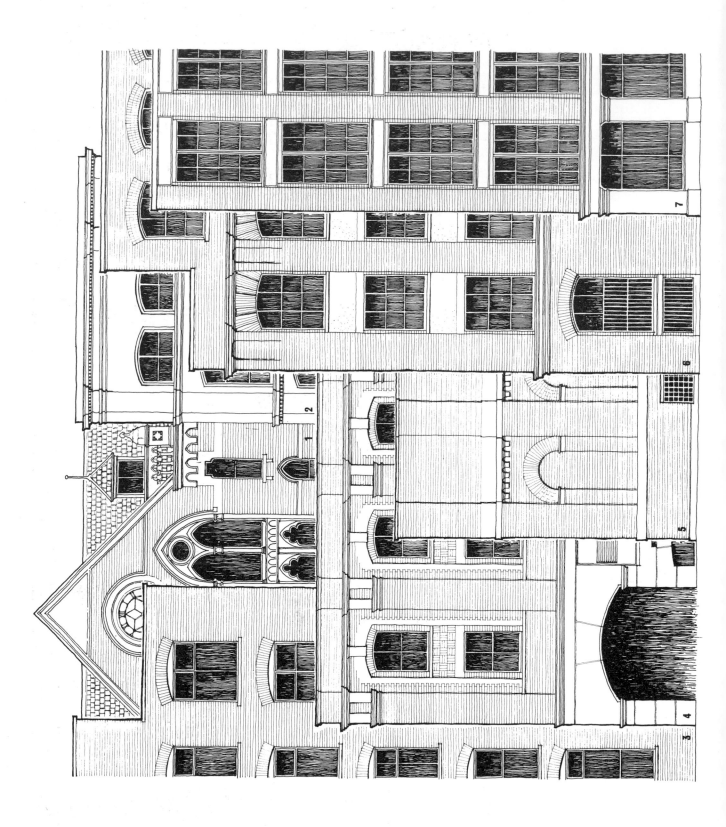

Plate 48

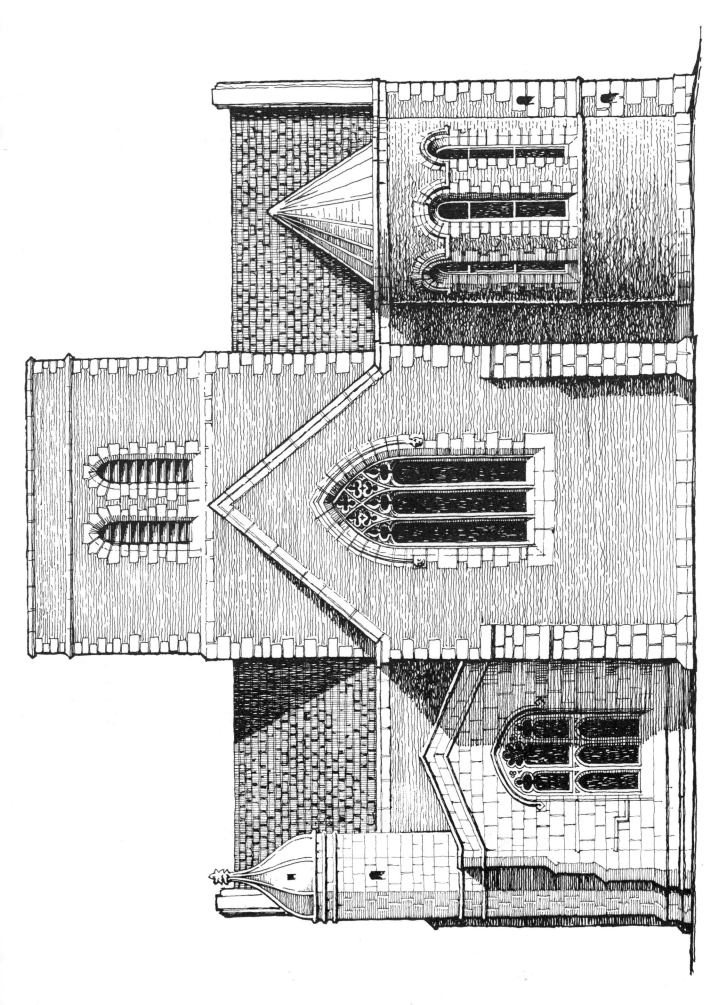

Plate 49

SCALE : ¾" TO 1'-0"

Plate 50

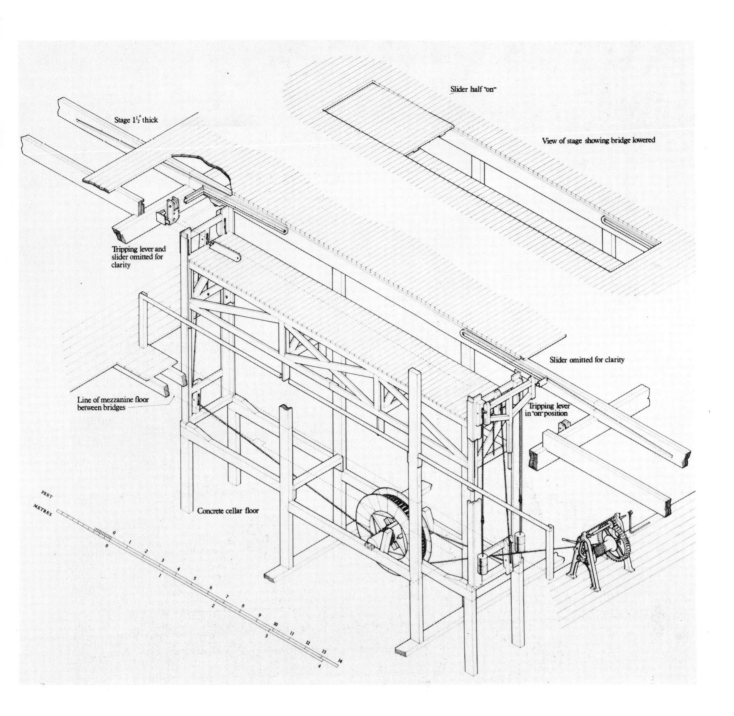

Slider half "on"

View of stage showing bridge lowered

Stage 1½" thick

Tripping lever and slider omitted for clarity

Slider omitted for clarity

Line of mezzanine floor between bridges

Tripping lever in "on" position

FEET

METRES

0 0 1 2 1 3 4 5 6 2 7 8 9 10 3 11 12 13 4 14

Concrete cellar floor

Plate 51   105

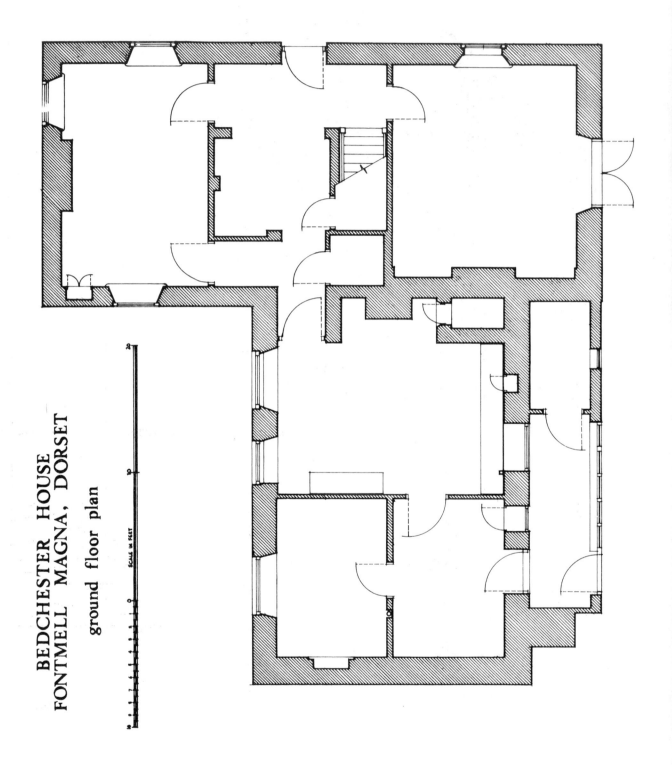

BEDCHESTER HOUSE
FONTMELL MAGNA, DORSET
ground floor plan

SCALE IN FEET

Plate 52

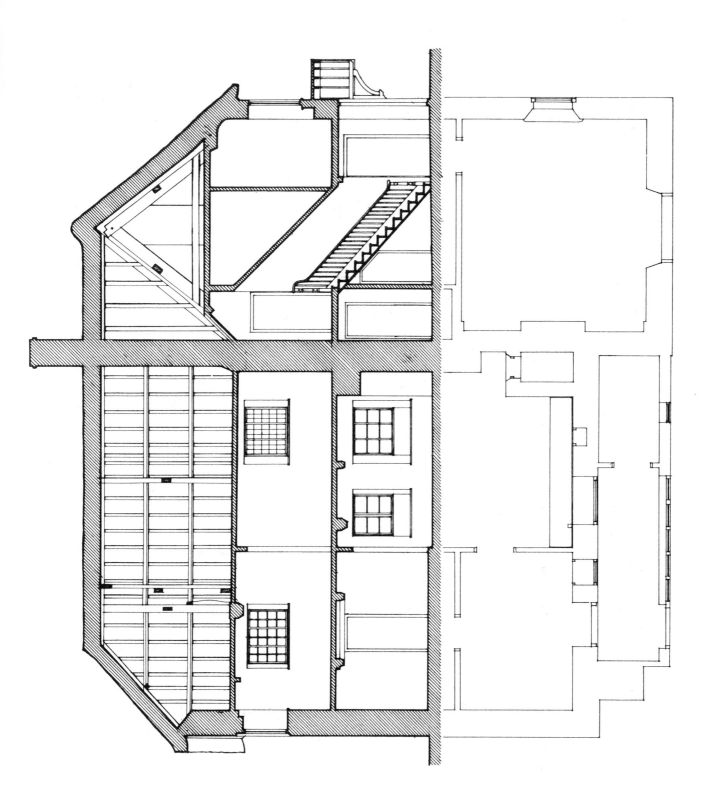

Plate 53

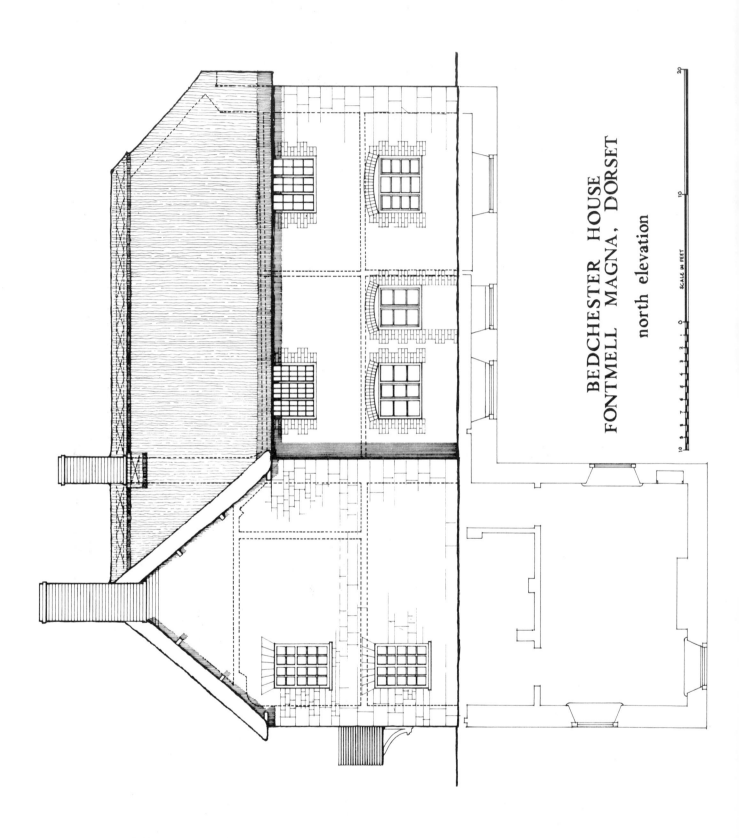

BEDCHESTER HOUSE
FONTMELL MAGNA, DORSET

north elevation

SCALE IN FEET

Plate 54

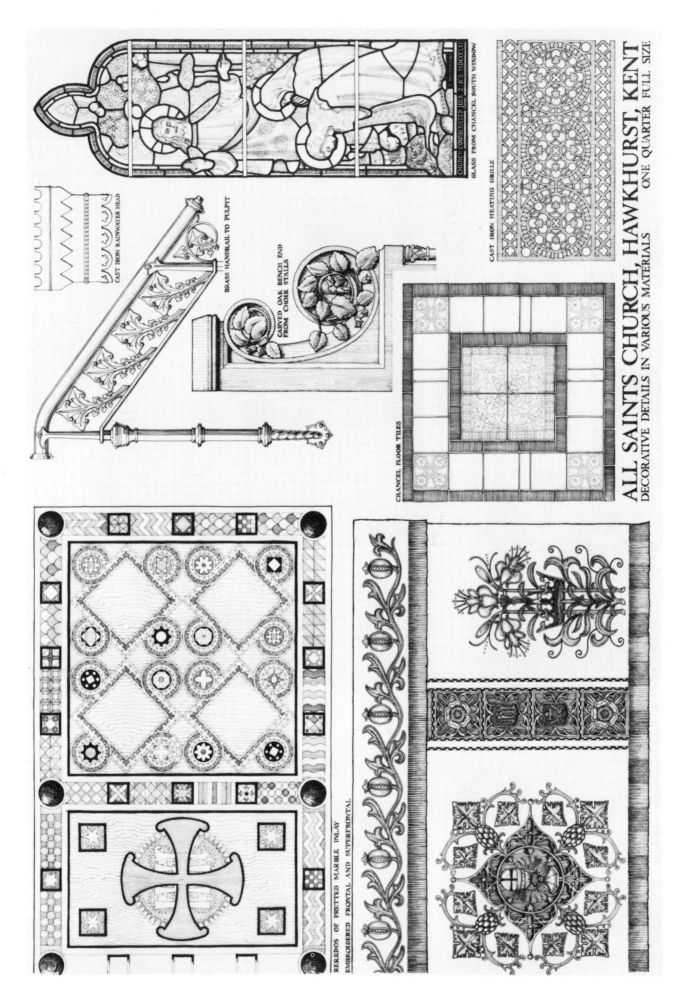

CAST IRON RAINWATER HEAD

BRASS HANDRAIL TO PULPIT

CARVED OAK BENCH END FROM CHOIR STALLS

GLASS FROM CHANCEL SOUTH WINDOW

CHURCH CONSECRATED JULY 2 A.D. MDCCCXLI

CAST IRON HEATING GRILLE

CHANCEL FLOOR TILES

REREDOS OF FRETTED MARBLE INLAY

EMBROIDERED FRONTAL AND SUPERFRONTAL

ALL SAINTS CHURCH, HAWKHURST, KENT

DECORATIVE DETAILS IN VARIOUS MATERIALS

ONE QUARTER FULL SIZE

Plate 55

109

110

Plate 56

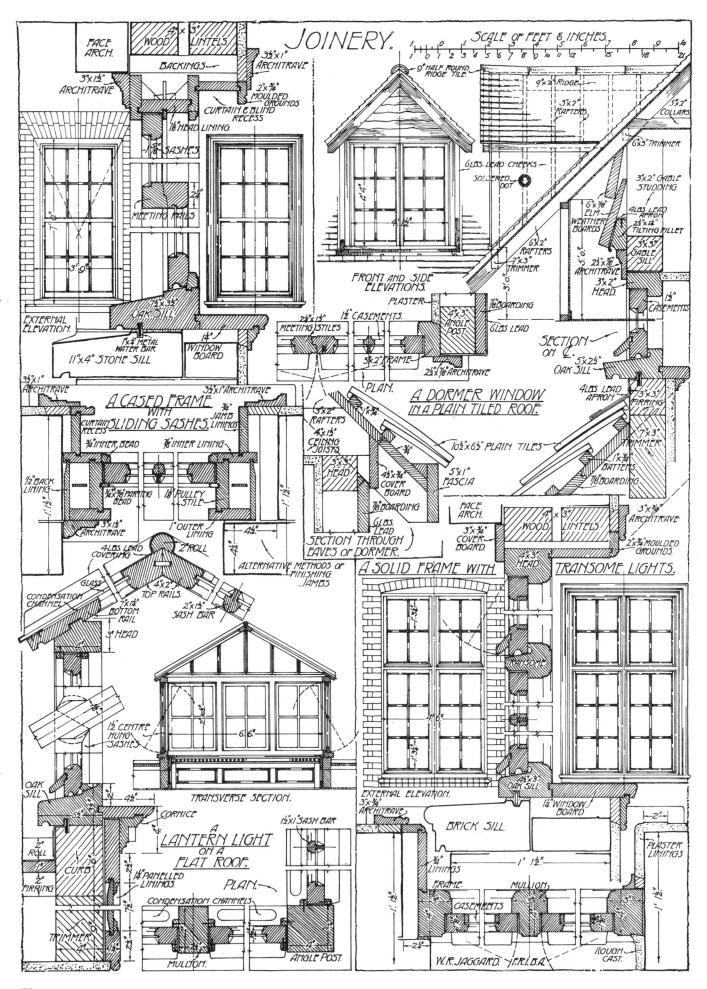

JOINERY.

SCALE OF FEET & INCHES.

FACE ARCH.
4" x 3" WOOD LINTELS
BACKINGS
3½" x 1" ARCHITRAVE
3" x 1½" ARCHITRAVE
2" x ¾" MOULDED GROUNDS
CURTAIN & BLIND RECESS
⅛" HEAD LINING
SASHES
MEETING RAILS
EXTERNAL ELEVATION.
OAK SILL
1" x ¼" METAL WATER BAR
WINDOW BOARD
11" x 4" STONE SILL

9" HALF ROUND RIDGE TILE.
9" x 2" RIDGE
3½" x 2" RAFTERS
5" x 2" COLLARS
6 LBS. LEAD CHEEKS
SOLDERED DOT
6" x 3" TRIMMER
3" x 2" GABLE STUDDING
6" x ⅞" ELM WEATHER BOARDS
4 LBS. LEAD APRON
2½" x 1¼" TILTING FILLET
3" x 3" GABLE SILL
2½" x ⅞" ARCHITRAVE
3" x 2" HEAD
CASEMENTS
FRONT AND SIDE ELEVATIONS.
6" x 2" RAFTERS
7" x 3" TRIMMER
SECTION ON C.
5" x 2½" OAK SILL

PLASTER
MEETING STILES
1½" CASEMENTS
2½" x 1½"
4" x 3" ANGLE POST
6 LBS. LEAD
7/8 BOARDING
PLAN.
3" x 2" FRAME
2½" x ⅞" ARCHITRAVE
A DORMER WINDOW IN A PLAIN TILED ROOF.

4 LBS. LEAD APRON
3" x 3" FIRRING
7½" x 3" TRIMMER
1" x ¾" BATTENS
7/8 BOARDING

A CASED FRAME WITH SLIDING SASHES.
3½" x 1" ARCHITRAVE
¾" JAMB LININGS
¾" INNER BEAD
7/8 INNER LINING
½" BACK LINING
¾" x ¾" PARTING BEAD
7/8 PULLEY STILE
3" x 1½" ARCHITRAVE
1" OUTER LINING
CURTAIN RECESS

5" x 2" RAFTERS
4" x 1½" CEILING JOISTS
3" x 3" HEAD
4½" x ¾" COVER BOARD
7/8 BOARDING
6 LBS. LEAD
SECTION THROUGH EAVES OF DORMER.
5" x 1" FASCIA
ALTERNATIVE METHODS OF FINISHING JAMBS

10½" x 6½" PLAIN TILES

FACE ARCH.
3" x ¾" COVER BOARD.
4" x 3" HEAD
4" x 3" WOOD LINTELS
3" x ¾" ARCHITRAVE
2" x ¾" MOULDED GROUNDS
A SOLID FRAME WITH TRANSOME LIGHTS.

4 LBS. LEAD COVERING
GLASS
CONDENSATION CHANNEL
7" x 1¼" BOTTOM RAIL
4" x 2" TOP RAILS
3" HEAD
2" x 1½" SASH BAR
1½" CENTRE HUNG SASHES
6. 6"
TRANSVERSE SECTION.
A LANTERN LIGHT ON A FLAT ROOF.
2" ROLL
CORNICE
OAK SILL
2" ROLL
CURB
1½" PANELLED LININGS
FIRRING
TRIMMER
CONDENSATION CHANNELS
1½" x 1" SASH BAR
PLAN.
MULLION.
ANGLE POST.

TRANSOME
4' 6"
EXTERNAL ELEVATION.
3" x ¾" ARCHITRAVE
BRICK SILL.
FRAME
LININGS
CASEMENTS
MULLION
4" x 3" OAK SILL
1¼" WINDOW BOARD
PLASTER LININGS
1' 1½"
ROUGH CAST.
W. R. JAGGARD. F.R.I.B.A.

Plate 57

111

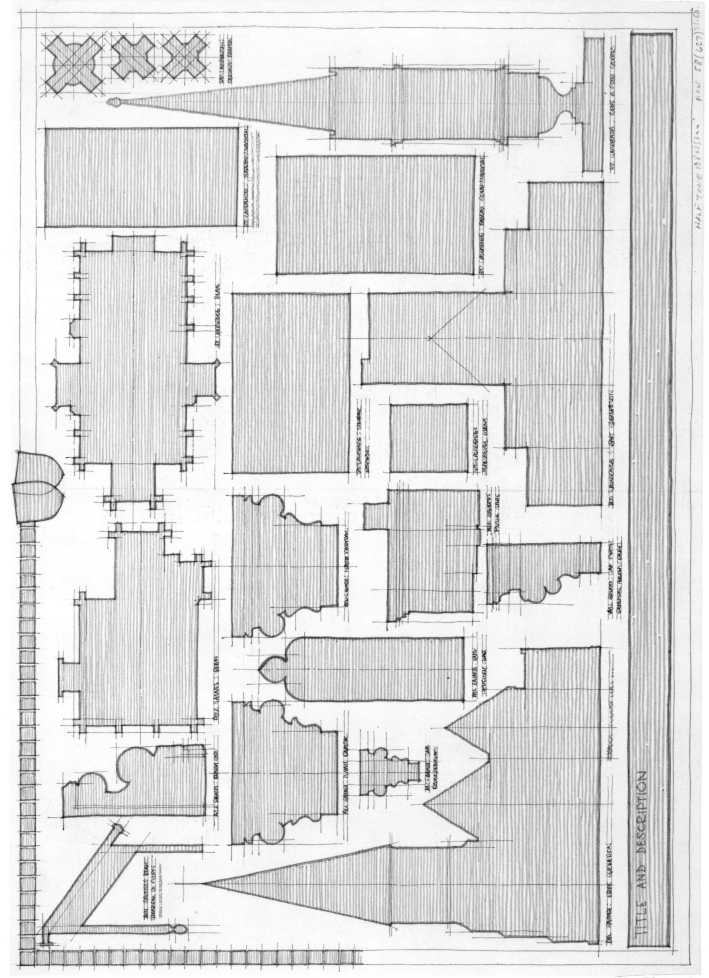

TITLE AND DESCRIPTION

Plate 58

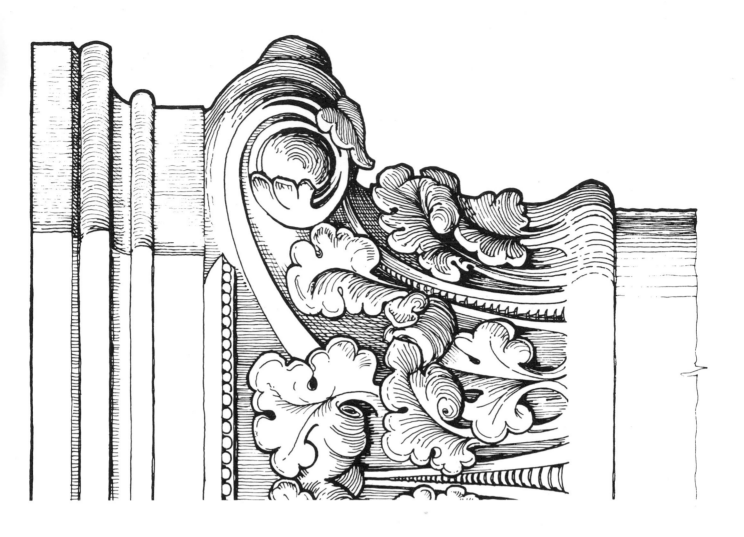

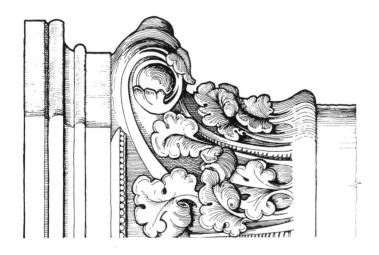

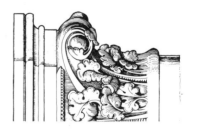

Plates 59, 60, 61

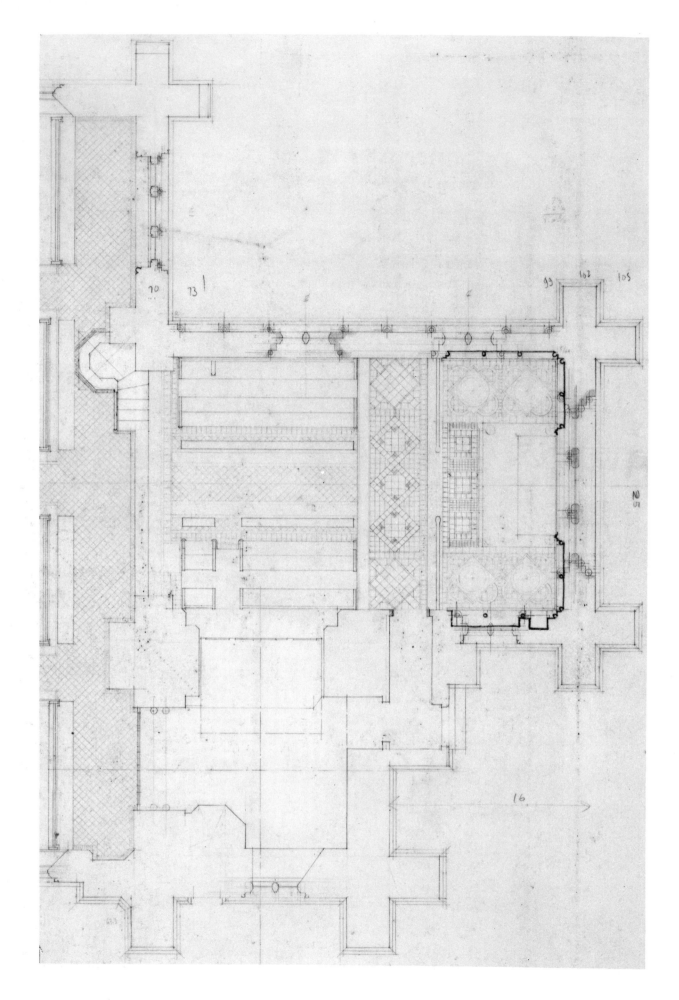

Plate 62

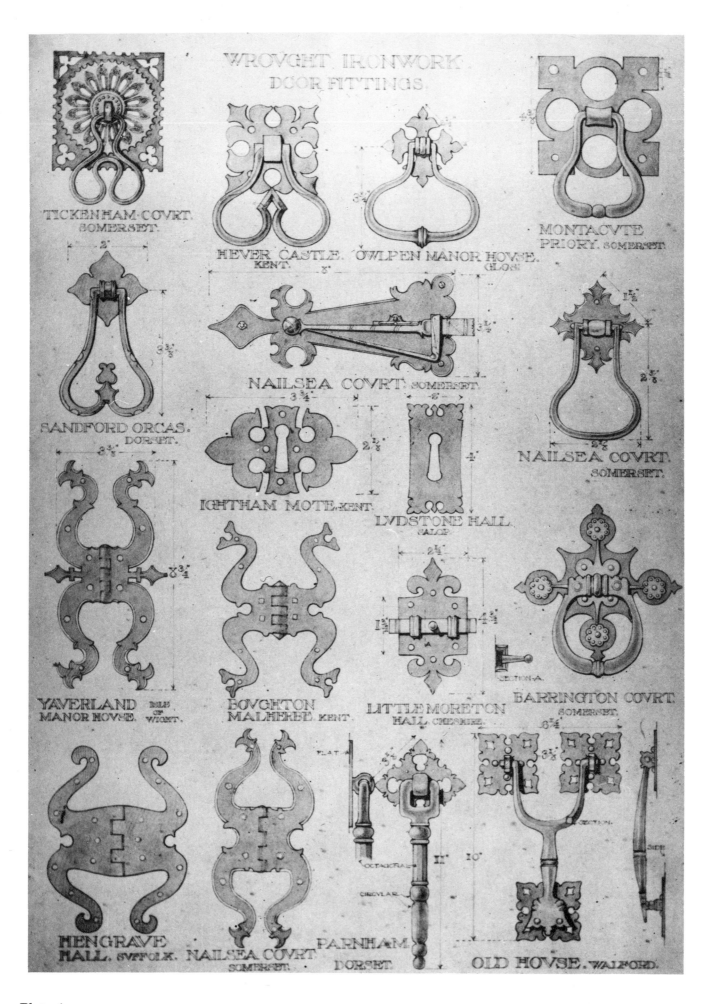

WROVGHT IRONWORK
DOOR FITTINGS

TICKENHAM COVRT.
SOMERSET.

HEVER CASTLE.
KENT.

OWLPEN MANOR HOVSE.
GLOS:

MONTACVTE
PRIORY. SOMERSET.

SANDFORD ORCAS.
DORSET.

NAILSEA COVRT. SOMERSET.

NAILSEA COVRT.
SOMERSET.

IGHTHAM MOTE. KENT.

LVDSTONE HALL.
SALOP.

YAVERLAND
MANOR HOVSE.
ISLE OF WIGHT.

BOVGHTON
MALHERBE. KENT.

LITTLE MORETON
HALL. CHESHIRE.

BARRINGTON COVRT.
SOMERSET.

HENGRAVE
HALL. SVFFOLK.

NAILSEA COVRT
SOMERSET.

PARNHAM
DORSET.

OLD HOVSE. WALFORD.

Plate 63

115

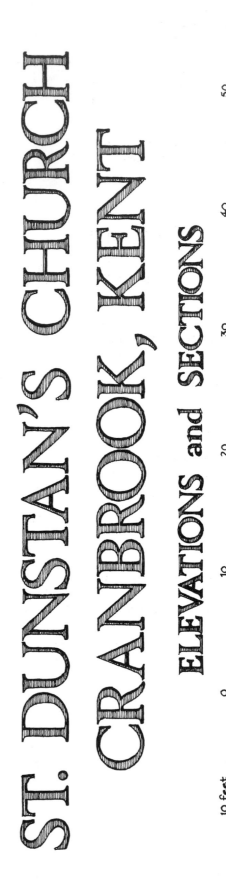

ST. DUNSTAN'S CHURCH
CRANBROOK, KENT

ELEVATIONS and SECTIONS

ST. DUNSTAN'S CHURCH
CRANBROOK, KENT

ELEVATIONS and SECTIONS

10 feet 0   10   20   30   40   50

TITLES.
Examples of serif & sans serif letter-forms:
1. Times New Roman.
2. Univers Medium.
Available in various sizes and weights in transfer lettering or type, or can be projected to the appropriate size and traced.

CAPTIONS.
Examples of styles for captions and annotations:
3. Serif.
4. Sans serif.

NUMBERS.
Numbers designed to align with top & bottom guidelines are less confusing than older style numbers with ascenders & descenders e.g:
5. Times.
6. Univers.
The decimal point should be centred in the depth of the figure (7), and fractions expressed using aligned figures with diagonal line to avoid excessive line depth.

SPACING.
Words are read as complete pictures and not as series of separate symbols. Good spacing is not achieved by equalising the linear distance between adjoining characters, but by equalising the areas of white between them.
8. Equal linear distance, and condensed letters, produce an uneven effect.
9. Extended spacing destroys the word-picture.
10. Even areas of white space between letters form coherent words.

MAIN HEADINGS.
Conventional Roman may be less effective than outline:
11. Modern Roman.
12. Egyptian.
13. Rockwell Slab Serif.
14. Condensed Sans Serif.
15. Sans Serif.
Bold faces, strong and readable from 25mm upwards, include:
16. Times Bold.
17. Univers Bold.

ABCDEFGHIJKLM
abcdefghijklm
NOPQRSTUVWXYZ
nopqrstuvwxyz
1

ABCDEFGHIJKLM
abcdefghijklm
NOPQRSTUVWXYZ
nopqrstuvwxyz
2

Detail of ceiling moulding for dining room
3

Detail of ceiling moulding for dining room
4

1234567890
5

1234567890
6

7 1·45 mm

½ 1/2

ELEVATIONANDPLAN
8

E L E V A T I O N
9

ELEVATION AND P
10

11 12 13 14 15

ABC
16

ABC
17

Plate 65

117

INDEX

NB Pages 39-42 MISSING!

9

WITHDRAWN